DO YOU HAVE THE "GREEN LIGHT" TO RETIRE?

How to Take Control of Your Finances for Your Future

TIMOTHY FITZWILLIAMS

with STEPHEN ROTH

Copyright © 2020 by Timothy Fitzwilliams

All rights reserved. No part of this publication may be reproduced, distributed or transmitted in any form or by any means, including photocopying, recording or other electronic or mechanical methods, without the prior written permission of the publisher, except in the case of brief quotations embodied in critical reviews and certain other noncommercial uses permitted by copyright law. For permission requests, write to the publisher at the address below. These materials are provided to you by Timothy Fitzwilliams for informational purposes only and Timothy Fitzwilliams expressly disclaims any and all liability arising out of or relating to your use of same. The provision of these materials does not constitute legal or investment advice and does not establish an attorney-client relationship between you and Timothy Fitzwilliams. No tax advice is contained in these materials. You are solely responsible for ensuring the accuracy and completeness of all materials as well as the compliance, validity and enforceability of all materials under any applicable law. The advice and strategies found within may not be suitable for every situation. You are expressly advised to consult with a qualified attorney or other professional in making any such determination and to determine your legal or financial needs. No warranty of any kind, implied, expressed or statutory, including but not limited to the warranties of title and non-infringement of third-party rights, is given with respect to this publication.

Timothy Fitzwilliams
Phone: 757.961.0700
Fax: 757.961.0701
Email: tim@ffinancial.net
Virginia Insurance License #127870

CHESAPEAKE OFFICE
860 Greenbrier Circle
Suite 305
Chesapeake, VA 23320

ISBN: 9798656759403

Fitzwilliams Financial is an independent financial services firm helping individuals create retirement strategies using a variety of insurance and investment products to custom suit their needs and objectives.

Neither the firm nor its agents or representatives may give tax or legal advice; however, Fitzwilliams Financial has a strategic partnership with tax professionals and attorneys who can provide these services. Individuals should consult with a qualified professional for guidance before making any purchasing decisions.

Insurance and annuity products offered through Fitzwilliams Financial Inc., VA Insurance License #127870.

Any references to protection benefits or steady and reliable income streams refer only to fixed insurance products. They do not refer, in any way, to securities or investment advisory products. Annuity guarantees are backed by the financial strength and claims-paying ability of the issuing insurance company. Annuities are insurance products that may be subject to fees, surrender charges and holding periods which vary by insurance company. Annuities are not FDIC insured. Investing involves risk, including possible loss of principal.

The information and opinions contained in this book are believed to be reliable, but accuracy and completeness cannot be guaranteed. They are given for informational purposes only and are not a solicitation to buy or sell any of the products mentioned. The information is not intended to be used as the sole basis for financial decisions, nor should it be construed as advice designed to meet the particular needs of an individual's situation.

The firm is not affiliated with the U.S. government or any governmental agency.

Table of Contents

INTRODUCTION I

TECHNOLOGY, TEMPTATION, AND TODAY'S CONSUMER 1

    CREDIT AND DEBIT CARDS 3

    ONLINE TRADING 6

    CONSTANT CONNECTIVITY 7

    THE "FUN" ACCOUNT 9

    STEPPING AWAY FROM TECHNOLOGY 11

A CRUCIAL TIME FOR YOUNG ADULTS 13

    WORKING WITHOUT A NET 16

    TAX-FREE RETIREMENT INCOME 17

    FOUR KINDS OF MONEY 18

    IRAS, ROTH IRAS, AND LIFE INSURANCE 20

    THE LIFE INSURANCE POLICY 22

    DON'T LOSE THE MONEY THROUGH TAXES! 24

FAMILY IS EVERYTHING 25

    A FAMILY APPROACH 27

    VALUE, ORDER AND PERSISTENCE 28

AMERICAN HUSTLE 31

"ALWAYS TAKE CARE OF FAMILY" 33

BASIC 401(K) MATH: "WHAT PERCENT IS IT?" 35

DO THE MATH 37

DON'T LET YOUR 401(K) JUST SIT THERE! 39

BORROWING AGAINST YOUR 401(K) 39

DO YOU HAVE A 401(K) COLLECTION? 40

SOCIAL SECURITY: WHEN SHOULD YOU TAKE IT? 45

SOCIAL SECURITY AND TAXATION 49

THE "TRANSFER ON DEATH" TRAP 55

OTHER THINGS TO KEEP IN MIND 57

THE TROUBLE WITH REQUIRED MINIMUM DISTRIBUTIONS 61

MANAGING YOUR RMDS 63

WHAT TO DO WITH RMD MONEY? 65

WHAT IF YOU NEED THE MONEY NOW? 66

LONG-TERM CARE: IT COULD HAPPEN TO YOU 69

THE COSTS OF LONG-TERM CARE 70

IS LONG-TERM CARE INSURANCE WORTH IT? 72

"IT'LL NEVER HAPPEN TO ME" 74

CLIMBING DOWN THE RETIREMENT MOUNTAIN— WITHOUT BREAKING YOUR NECK! 79

    THREE IMPORTANT QUESTIONS 82

    WHAT'S THE RIGHT ANSWER? 83

    THE RIGHT PATH DOWN THE MOUNTAIN 83

DON'T WAIT, DON'T PROCRASTINATE! 85

    THE BUYER'S MARKET OF 1803 87

    THOSE WHO IGNORE HISTORY… 88

    ARE YOU A "MACARTHUR?" 90

    AGAIN, DON'T PROCRASTINATE! 93

THERE'S NO "I" IN "TEAM" 95

    THE JORDAN RULES 96

    IT TAKES A TEAM 97

    BUILDING THE FITZWILLIAMS FINANCIAL TEAM 99

    GATHERING THE BEST TEAM 104

THE GREEN-LIGHT RETIREMENT 107

    A HOLISTIC APPROACH TO RETIREMENT 108

    RED LIGHT, GREEN LIGHT 110

    THE ULTIMATE GOAL? A BALANCED APPROACH 113

ABOUT THE AUTHOR 117
ACKNOWLEDGMENTS 119
CONTACT US 121

Introduction

I remember it like it was yesterday.

I'm eight years old, staring down the hallway of our beautiful home in Virginia Beach's Broad Bay Island. My grandmother is at the other end of that hallway, and she won't tell me where my mom has gone. I keep asking her, but she won't tell me.

I know that my dad, John Fitzwilliams, had gone on a business trip the week before, but that doesn't explain my mom's sudden disappearance. Finally after several minutes of questioning (even back then, I was extremely persistent), my grandmother gives in and tells me, calmly, that Mom had to leave to be with my dad this morning because he'd had a massive heart attack and needed immediate quadruple bypass surgery.

My father survived that surgery, but his health was never the same. That morning with my grandmother in 1987 was a turning point for my family, and not in a good way.

Fast-forward a few years. I'm eleven or twelve years old, in junior high school, and starting to get involved in after-school activities. For some reason during this time, I'm always the last kid to be picked up in front of my school. I hate waiting around for my mother to show up in her car.

One day, finally, I ask why she's always late—and that's how I learn my mom has come down with breast cancer. She's getting radiation treatments while I'm busy with junior high wrestling and choir.

My parents' poor health created a lot of distress, agony and pain for my family. Unfortunately, it took a toll on our finances as well. We eventually lost that pretty home at Broad Bay Island, and my family had to start from scratch. With two sick parents, I was often enlisted to help them run our family business, JLT Associates.

Today, I'm forty years old, living in an established neighborhood with a "mother-in-law suite" out back for my mom. For several years, she shared that suite with my dad, who had come down with dementia. Every day with my father's dementia was a struggle for our family. In March of 2019, he passed away at the hospital, and I watched my mom's income diminish once again.

I'm sharing these experiences with you not to build sympathy, but to explain why financial management and retirement planning are so deeply important to me. I have seen, first-hand, what can happen when life events spiral out of control, eating away at savings and financial security. I know from my own experience the effects that poor health and insufficient planning can have on every member of a family, and how the breadwinners of that family can spend the rest of their lives just trying to make ends meet.

That's why, in 2008, I started Fitzwilliams Financial, a practice dedicated to helping people prepare and save for successful retirements. I wanted my clients to not just endure the often stressful transition from working life to the "golden years." I wanted them to realize the retirement of their dreams, whether that meant moving to a warmer climate, starting a new business, or playing golf four times a week.

Fitzwilliams Financial was not an overnight success, and I experienced a few financial challenges of my own (we'll get to some of those later). By 2009, though, my business was on firm footing, and I was able to start building a ten-person team with expertise in areas like investing, estate planning, insurance, and other legal and financial instruments.

As a former economics major from George Mason University, I'm just smart enough to know I can't be an expert on every layer of finances. In fact, I'm not good at a lot of things. Not even close. So, I've assembled a team to advise our clients through the many twists and turns of financial management and life events. In today's complex world, with so many financial products, and the power to make critical financial decisions with just a mouse-click, it's more important than ever to have a well-coordinated team of professionals in your corner. No one can know all this stuff in a vacuum. It's just not possible.

Today, in addition to my regular duties at Fitzwilliams Financial, I host a Saturday radio show (appropriately called *Don't Lose the Money*), as well as numerous dinner seminars in some of the finest area restaurants throughout the year. I've written articles about retirement, annuities and income protection for publications like *Fortune* magazine and *CNN Money*. I've been interviewed and featured on Fox News, CNN, and CNBC.

The radio show, news articles and seminars are great marketing tools for Fitzwilliams Financial, of course, but they're also an effective way for me to interact with a wide range of people, and learn more about their perspectives and challenges in approaching retirement.

One thing that strikes me about these interactions with people is how many of them truly believe that, because they are successful in their careers, they are automatically experts at budgeting, investing, saving and planning for a successful retirement. In my experience, that is very rarely the case. Positioning yourself for retirement takes a different set of skills and knowledge base. Even if you're making good money right now, that doesn't necessarily ensure that you and your spouse will be sipping piña coladas and watching the sun set over the ocean ten, twenty or thirty years from now.

That's why I wrote this book. I wanted a physical product that contained the more common pitfalls and adversities of retirement planning, as well as time-tested strategies to help you dodge those traps along the way. I wanted people to walk away from my seminars and one-on-one sessions with a customized roadmap for plotting a successful retirement. The seminars that Fitzwilliams Financial hosts are lively, interactive affairs, but the ideas we share can fade from memory after a few days. This book digs deeper into those seminar topics, and you can pull it off the shelf at any time for a quick refresher on financial planning.

In short, I want this book to be a trusted tool for anyone who dreams of walking away from work with ample savings, a solid plan in place, and assets to pass along to their children. That's what I want for my family, and that's what I wish could have been provided for my mother and father.

Financial health, like physical health, isn't something you can take for granted. Fortunately, though, there are things you can do to prepare for anything life throws at you.

CHAPTER ONE

Technology, Temptation, and Today's Consumer

You don't have to read a book to know that technology has come a long way over the past two decades. Each of us has come to rely on technology every day in ways we never could have imagined a few years ago. We turn to our smartphones, tablets and other digital devices for information, entertainment, to make transactions and to keep in touch with friends and family.

The richness and immediacy of today's consumer technology is truly amazing. However, it can come at a cost. Depending too much on your devices to make everyday decisions can be a big mistake. Often, we don't realize how our phones and the Internet affect our behavior until it's too late. Easy access to credit lines, debit cards, online trading, and other financial instruments doesn't help, either.

Here's a little story to illustrate how much technology has changed.

It's 1985. Ronald Reagan is president, Microsoft has released its first version of Windows, and the biggest cultural event of the year is the Live Aid benefit concert for Ethiopia. In other words, it's a long, long time ago.

Around this time my mother and father decide to sell their shares of Coca-Cola stock, because they're a little uncomfortable with this New Coke formula the company just rolled out. My mom picks up the phone, the one with the long, spiral cord she sometimes raps me with when I come home from playing too late. She calls her broker and orders the sale of the Coke stock. It's 4:30 p.m. on Friday. The stock market is already closed, so the broker can't call in the sale until Monday morning.

My parents have more than two days to think over their decision to sell the stock. On Sunday, they decide that maybe New Coke isn't so bad, and they'll hold onto to their Coca-Cola shares for a little bit longer. My mom calls the broker again, and leaves a message on his answering machine not to sell. The broker gets the message Monday morning, and the stock does not sell.

Fast-forward thirty-five years to today. I have a day-trading account. It's 8:30 p.m. and I want to sell some Apple stock. I get on my phone and say, "Siri, sell 500 shares of Apple stock." Just like that—finger snap!—it's gone. The shares are sold, and I can't get them back. I didn't have to make a phone call or wait an extra day to do it.

The point of my story is that the real-time accessibility of digital technology and products can sometimes lead to quick, regrettable decisions. We all know people who got mad and decided to spout off on Facebook or Twitter, and then got pummeled for that decision over the next several hours or days.

What if, instead of firing off an unwise comment on social media, you make a hasty online transaction that hurts you financially, and that you'll later regret? Impulsive decision-making happens all the time these days because it's so easy to do. And once you make that mouse-click or tell your digital assistant what you want done, there is no recourse.

I know a woman who decided to buy $1,000 worth of a cannabis company stock on the Internet. The only problem was that she accidentally purchased 1,000 shares of the stock, which was several thousand dollars more than she intended to spend. Unfortunately, there was nothing she could do to correct her mistake. The stock sale went through, and that was that.

I believe this kind of impulsive decision-making is a big reason why American consumers are once again up to their eyeballs in debt, after a brief decline following the Great Recession of 2008-09. According to Federal Reserve data, the total amount of revolving credit debt in the United States surpassed $1 trillion in 2017, the first time that's happen since George W. Bush was president.[1] Some of the lessons of the last recession, apparently, have been forgotten by many consumers.

Below are three key developments in technology and finance that have helped fuel all that spending and borrowing, followed by two solutions that can help you avoid these common financial mistakes.

Credit and Debit Cards

The convenience of plastic debit and credit cards means that few Americans carry cash anymore. A recent survey of 1,000 consumers

---

[1] Maria LaMagna. MarketWatch. August 8, 2017. "Americans now have the highest credit card debt in U.S. history."
https://www.marketwatch.com/story/us-households-will-soon-have-as-much-debt-as-they-had-in-2008-2017-04-03

by DepositAccounts.com found that one in three of them would have to hit up an ATM machine just to make a $20 cash payment. Nearly 35 percent of the youngest respondents said they never carry cash at all.[2]

In a 2018 survey of 1,200 consumers by TSYS, a payment processing service, 54 percent of respondents said they prefer to make payments with debit cards, 26 percent preferred credit cards, and only 14 percent favored cash.[3] Why have cash when you can pay for nearly anything by inserting or swiping a plastic card?

The disadvantage, of course, is that plastic makes it incredibly easy to overspend. If you have $20 in your pocket, and nothing else, you know that your purchasing power at that moment is limited to $20. If you carry a debit or credit card, there is little transparency to how much money you really have, and how much you can afford to spend. And, if you have a $5,500 line of credit handy, you may not even care at that moment—until you get your monthly credit card bill.

Banks and credit card companies capitalize on this free-and-easy spending through interest rates and overdraft fees. It's a booming business. Credit card lending grew to more than $900 billion in 2018, according to the Consumer Financial Protection Bureau. The credit card market spiked in 2008, before the Great Recession encouraged consumers to pull back on their spending. That bout of

---

[2] Lauren Perez. DepositAccounts. August 20, 2019. "1 in 3 Americans Can't Make a $20 Cash Purchase Without Using an ATM." https://www.depositaccounts.com/blog/carrying-cash.html

[3] Jason Steele. CreditCards.com. May 9, 2019. "Payment Method Statistics." https://www.creditcards.com/credit-card-news/payment-method-statistics-1276.php

thriftiness only lasted a few years, as credit card lending has steadily increased since 2015.[4]

Meanwhile, banks are making a killing on overdraft fees when customers spend beyond their means. The average overdraft fee has increased from $21.57 in 1998 to $33.23 in 2018, according to Bankrate.com.[5] Credit Union fees have also risen, from $15 in 2000 to $29 today. More consumers are overdrawing on their bank accounts, as overdraft fees totaled more than $34.3 billion in 2017, the most since 2009, according to Moebs Services.[6]

Many bank customers are automatically enrolled in overdraft protection services, which means the bank will cover a big transaction even if the customer has insufficient funds. That, of course, leads to the overdraft fee. Most customers would probably be better off being declined on a purchase they don't have enough money to make. But overdraft protection encourages irresponsible spending, and banks have found a way to profit from it.

---

[4] Consumer Financial Protection Bureau. Banking Journal. August 27, 2019. "CFPB: Total Credit Card Balances Reach $900B in 2018."
https://bankingjournal.aba.com/2019/08/total-credit-card-balances-reach-900b-in-2018/

[5] Amanda Dixon. Bankrate. October 10, 2018. "Survey: ATM fees hit a record high for the 14th year in a row."
https://www.bankrate.com/banking/checking/checking-account-survey-2018/?itm_source=parsely-api?relsrc=parsely

[6] Julia Chang. Learnvest in Forbes. April 5, 2018. "Americans Paid $34 Billion in Overdraft Fees Last Year. Here's How to Stop the Charges."
https://www.forbes.com/sites/learnvest/2018/04/05/americans-paid-34-billion-in-overdraft-fees-last-year-heres-how-to-stop-the-charges/#735980573ce9

Online Trading

A little history: After the stock market crashed in 1987, the Securities and Exchange Commission took steps to protect smaller investors who were unable to call in stock sales during the crash. The newly formed Small Order Entry System gave orders of 1,000 shares or less a priority over larger orders.

This change not only protected small-time, individual investors, it also removed a barrier to entry into the stock market, and opened the doors to more investors than ever before. Soon, Internet day trading services like E-Trade made it even easier for individuals to directly buy and sell shares. This phenomenon helped fuel the bull market of the 1990s. I believe that it also led to a herd mentality among amateur investors that inflated tech stock prices and then helped cause the dot-com bubble to burst in 2000.

Today, buying and selling stocks is even easier and more efficient. As I mentioned, gone are the days when you had to call your broker and wait a day for the transaction to go through.

The ease of trading and the unprecedented number of investors in the public markets have led to much greater market uncertainty, in my opinion, simply because there are more people able to actively participate. If you look at the charts from 2000 until today, you'll see that there is a heightened volatility in trading.

That, I believe, is the effect of modern technology and communications. We live in a world where one presidential tweet can mean a 200-point drop in the Dow Jones Industrial Average within minutes. Likewise, investors can read an alarming story on their Google newsfeed, and sell off shares of a related stock instantaneously.

You don't even have to be a talking-head expert like Jim Cramer to move the market. Would it shock anyone if Kim Kardashian one day tweeted a mirror selfie with her new Android phone, and inadvertently sparked a sell-off of Apple stock?

These are the absurd times we live in, and the loser isn't Wall Street. It's everyday consumers and retirees who suffer hits to their portfolios because a Kardashian decides she likes Android phones more than Apple.

Constant Connectivity

Like a lot of men my age, I love video games. I'm a gamer, and the amount of time I spend down in the man cave/family game room playing online games like *Call of Duty* and *Madden NFL* is a little more than I would care to admit.

Because I love the exhilaration and competition of video games, I'm sometimes tempted to buy new games or features on the spot. If you play games online, you understand the constant bombardment of ads and promotions that urge you to upgrade your avatar or download a new game. There are probably about five million games out there I could download right now.

Gaming is a huge business, estimated to exceed $32 billion by 2025, according to ResearchandMarkets.com.[7] It's also a huge hustle.

---

[7] BusinessWire. September 3, 2019. "Global Gamification Market Anticipated to Exceed $32 Billon by 2025-ResearchAndMarkets.com"

People spend thousands and thousands of real dollars on little pixels for their game avatars. I can relate somewhat to that passion. Do I really need a new weapon or suit of armor for my character on Fortnite? Not really. But sometimes, I might give in to that temptation.

That's one example of the deluge of marketing messages we are subjected to on a daily basis because of our constant connectivity through smartphones, tablets and home computers. Digital experts estimate that most Americans are exposed to between 4,000 and 10,000 advertisements per day.[8] That's a lot of information to say "no" to. And with artificial intelligence and Internet algorithms growing more sophisticated, those ads are becoming more personalized and targeted to your needs and wants. Sooner or later, they'll hit on something you just can't resist.

Internet advertising, of course, draws on data collected from our Google search histories and social media activity. Currently, there are an estimated 3.5 billion social media users worldwide, or about 45 percent of the world population. And that number, despite your Aunt Linda's determination to delete her Facebook account, is constantly growing.[9]

---

https://www.businesswire.com/news/home/20190903005426/en/Global-Gamification-Market-Anticipated-Exceed-32-Billion

[8] Ryan Holmes. LinkedIn. February 19, 2019. "We Now See 5,000 Ads a Day . . . And It's Getting Worse." https://www.linkedin.com/pulse/have-we-reached-peak-ad-social-media-ryan-holmes

[9] Linday Tjepkema. Emarsys. January 3, 2019. "Top 5 Social Media Predictions for 2019." https://emarsys.com/learn/blog/top-5-social-media-predictions-2019/

Tell me if this scenario sounds familiar? You're in the market for a new car, and you're especially interested in a Honda CR-V. You've probably talked this over with your spouse or friends, asking them what kind of car they recommend. You log onto your Facebook account to look at cute pet and baby photos, and there it is: an Internet ad for 2019 CR-Vs at your nearest Honda dealership. How on earth did they know? Are you being spied on? Was someone listening in on your phone conversation?

It's doubtful that Big Brother was listening in, and more likely that the algorithm was advanced enough to pick up on your interest in Hondas. Any digital conversation you might have had about your car search can be drawn upon by advertisers for marketing purposes.

This may sound spooky or cool, depending on your view of technology. Ultimately, our constant connectivity and aggressive promotions from advertisers can lead to impulsive, ill-timed buying decisions. The immediacy and power of interactive technology is amazing, but it can ruin how consumers manage and look at their budgets.

Fortunately, there are a couple of tactics you can use to effectively combat all of this.

The "Fun" Account

Things move fast today. The constant flow of information can lead to some regrettable decisions. Preventing those mistakes requires more than just balancing your checkbook every month. You need a living, breathing plan for budgeting and money management. Without it, your spending and financial security can quickly spiral out of control.

Fortunately, I have a suggestion for one option that allows you to maintain control, one I often share with audiences at my seminars.

The suggestion is this: Take a look at your family's monthly income—your take-home pay. Subtract from that income your monthly bills—your mortgage, car payments, cable bill and any other fixed costs.

How much income remains after you pay those expenses? Let's say, for the sake of simplicity, you have $1,000 left over every month after paying your bills. Take that $1,000, and split it in half. You put $500 of that money away, preferably in something sensible like a Roth IRA or another retirement account.

The balance of that money—the other $500—goes into your "fun" account. It's yours to spend on anything you want that month—movies, sporting events, fine dining or even (ahem!) video games. Whatever you want. It doesn't matter how you spend that money. It's for you to enjoy.

What's important is that you pay close attention to your income and costs, and actually have a separate bank account for your "fun" money. Without the separate account, it's very easy to go astray in your spending.

Consistently compartmentalizing your money into separate accounts is easy to do and can lead to savvier, more thoughtful financial decisions. Let's say you find a deal on a new refrigerator for $100 a month, zero-interest, for eighteen months. A brand-new, stainless steel kitchen appliance would be nice, but that $100 will have to come from your monthly fun account. You may have to decide what's more important over the next year-and-a-half: a new fridge with extra freezer space, or taking the family to see the latest Marvel superhero movie every single month?

Armed with the knowledge of exactly how much disposable income you and your family have to spend, you can make stronger purchasing decisions. But it takes a disciplined, old-school approach to budgeting and iron-will determination to ignore those thousands of ads on TV and the Internet that you see every day.

Which gets me to my next solution:

Stepping Away From Technology

Most of us need technology in our lives to make money, interact with friends and family, and know what's going on in the world. It's important to stay connected and, for many of us, digital communication, automation, and other advances have made our lives significantly better.

But, do we need to consume technology and media every single day, all day long? Do we need for our smartphones to be the last thing we see before we go to bed, and the first thing we see when we wake up?

I don't think we do. In fact, studies have shown that taking a break every now and then from the constant flow of information, breaking news and marketing messages can make us happier and more well-balanced. According to a long-range study by the University of Montreal, families who have high-quality—including device-free—environment dinners together most days of the week tend to have children who are healthier, more confident, and less likely to smoke, use drugs or drink alcohol.[10] That's just one example of how taking a small break from technology, and interacting with your loved ones, can have far-reaching positive effects on your life.

I believe managing how we consume information and technology can lead to sounder financial decisions and less impulsiveness. But, as with the "fun" budget, you have to make a conscious effort to step away. Maybe you unplug from technology during your family dinners. Maybe, when you get home from work each night, you put that phone away and try not to look at it until you leave home the next morning. Sound impossible? Somehow, you managed to do it in 2007 before the iPhone came out. Try it again, and see what happens.

The Norwegian politician and Nobel Prize winner Christian Lous Lange once said, "Technology is a useful servant, but a dangerous master." He said that in 1921, by the way, but those words ring true today.

Is technology your servant, or your master? By consistently managing your exposure to it and knowing how it affects your behavior, you can make technology work for you instead of the other way around.

---

[10] Marie-Josée Harbec, Linda S. Pagani. *Journal of Developmental & Behavioral Pediatrics*. 2017. "Associations Between Early Family Meal Environment Quality and Later Well-Being in School-Age Children." https://www.sciencedaily.com/releases/2017/12/171214092322.htm

CHAPTER TWO

A Crucial Time for Young Adults

Maintaining a budget and living within one's means are particularly crucial for younger adults in their twenties and thirties.

The reason: They have less of a margin for error than older adults. The number of economic forces working against them are astounding: student debt, underemployment, less job security, the skyrocketing cost of health care, the decline of pensions and a drying up of Social Security funding are just a few of the challenges millennials face as they plan for retirement.

Of course, millennials have themselves to blame for a few of their hardships. Like older consumers, many young adults spend way beyond their means and immerse themselves in mindless, nonproductive activities. Their spending habits are different, though. Instead of paying too much for a $45,000 SUV or a $1 million McMansion, they're blowing their savings on comfort items like $5 coffees, the latest tech gadgets, and Uber rides.

There's nothing wrong with the finer things in life, right? But younger adults, perhaps more than the generations before them, have a tendency to spend in the moment without thinking much about how they're going to pay off their credit card bill later in the month.

At the end of 2018, debt among nineteen- to twenty-nine-year-old Americans surpassed $1 trillion, according to the New York Federal Reserve. That's an awful lot of Iced Caffe Lattes. It's also the highest level of debt for young adults since 2007.[11]

I'm not exactly young anymore, but I try to keep up with trends. I talk to kids and young adults all the time. I'll see some kid who's right out of college and he's getting a new 4K ultra HD television set at Best Buy. I wonder to myself, does that young man have the kind of money to afford a $1,400 Samsung, or is he just trying to keep up with his friends?

What many young adults don't understand is that some of the smartest marketing and financial people in the world are bombarding them every day with schemes geared toward capturing their last dollar. A common hustle is the cell phone plan agreement, promising unlimited data and technology upgrades for up to $100 per month. How many people in their twenties and early thirties can afford to carry around the latest smartphone technology? How many of them actually need that kind of a phone plan?

In addition to being saddled with debt—much of it from unpaid college loans—many young adults have unrealistic expectations on how to get out from under that debt. It's not as simple as starting a GoFundMe page, a Patreon account or making a YouTube video. I spoke with a young man the other day who boasted about the millions of dollars he could make by being a video game YouTuber.

---

[11] Alexandre Tanzi. *Bloomberg*. February 25, 2019. "Millennials Are Facing $1 Trillion in Debt." https://www.bloomberg.com/news/articles/2019-02-25/millennials-face-1-trillion-debt-as-student-loans-pile-up

Usually, when I hear something ridiculous, I keep my mouth shut. But in the face of this kind of neon-red ignorance on stilts, I could not resist telling the young man that, no, YouTubing your video games is not a $1 billion-plus plan. You'd be lucky to make $100,000 doing that, and only if you're a gaming rock star.

My point is, many young adults' mindset about money is, "I'll come up with something later," or "I'll put that off for another day." The problems occur when a day turns into weeks, then months, then years. The next thing you know, you're seventy years old and working at Walmart and wondering "What happened?"

There's also an air of victimhood with younger adults that I find a little bit disturbing. Sure, they've had some tough breaks, but a heightened level of sensitivity isn't going to help them navigate an increasingly difficult economy.

Case in point: Some nights, after my kids are in bed, I like to play video games. Often, I'm communicating with other gamers through a voice and text chat called Discord. One evening recently, there was a disagreement over a particular game in our forum, and one of the gamers started complaining about a "negative energy" in our chat room.

I'm incredulous. Is this person serious? Who on earth gets upset about the negative energy of an online chat among strangers? And if you don't like the way a conversation's going, why not just log off?

My point is, young adults simply can't afford to have such fragile psyches, especially given the financial obstacles that stand in their path.

Working Without a Net

One of those challenges is Social Security. Much has been written about the dire future of our social safety net. The Transamerica Center for Retirement Studies showed that an increasing number of workers distrust whether Social Security benefits will be there for them, a top retirement-related concern, even as most survey respondents also said they expected to rely in whole or in part on those same benefits.[12]

Even the Social Security Administration agrees that things look bleak, without a sudden windfall of more funding. Here's what the government writes on your annual Social Security statement:

"Without changes, in 2033, the Social Security Trust Fund will be able to pay only about 75 cents for each dollar of scheduled benefits. We need to resolve these issues soon to make sure Social Security continues to provide a foundation of protection for future generations."

The year 2033 is just a little more than a decade a way. Today's nineteen- to twenty-nine-year-olds won't reach retirement age for nearly forty years. What percentage of Social Security will remain for that generation, without quick and decisive action from our nation's leaders?

---

[12] Transamerica Center for Retirement Studies. June 2018. "18th Annual Transamerica Retirement Survey."
https://www.transamericacenter.org/docs/default-source/retirement-survey-of-workers/tcrs2018_sr_18th_annual_worker_compendium.pdf

What I advise people in their twenties and thirties about Social Security is simple: "Pretend it's not there." Because, the way things are going, it just might not be.

Of course, that means young people will have to be especially careful in planning their retirements. One essential strategy, in addition to disciplined budgeting and saving, is to reduce one's tax exposure as much as possible. Proper execution of this strategy could shield a significant chunk of your savings from Uncle Sam. Here's some ideas to do this:

Tax-Free Retirement Income

So, Social Security is in trouble. The national debt is growing at a faster pace than ever before—to more than $23 *trillion* in early 2020. When you factor in Social Security, Medicare and other government programs committed to, but not paid for, that debt escalates. USDebtClock.org puts the budget deficit, or the difference between the U.S. tax revenue and what Congress approved for the annual budget at more than $1 trillion just for this year. And right now, thanks to the Trump tax cuts that went into effect in 2018, the federal marginal tax rates are at the lowest levels they've been since the pre-New Deal days of the 1920s.

In the midst of this lopsided financial condition, something eventually has got to give. Despite the reluctance of our elected officials to accept responsibility, sooner or later they are going to have to raise federal taxes, something that hasn't been done since the first term of the Clinton Administration.

When that happens—and I believe it will eventually happen—the impact of taxation on the retirement savings of working and middle class Americans could be significant. Young adults, many who may only be starting to think about saving for their retirements, are particularly at risk.

For this reason, it's important to have a plan in place that limits your savings' tax exposure as much as possible. Fortunately, there are a few financial instruments in place that you can use to this end.

The famously wise businessman, investor and philanthropist Warren Buffett had it right when he shared his two rules of investing: "Rule No. 1: Never lose money; Rule No. 2: Never forget Rule No. 1."

Hey, there's a reason they call him the Oracle of Omaha!

The simplicity of Buffett's "two" rules is at the heart of receiving tax free retirement income. This approach is designed to shield as much of your retirement savings from taxation (ie: "losing the money") as possible. In this way, you can replace much of what you may or may not be getting from a depleted Social Security net.

Four Kinds of Money

In adopting a tax-free income approach, you should look at your money in four different ways:

1. **Free Money**: This is money that's been given to you, like an inheritance or an employer's matching contribution to your 401(k) plan. It's free money you didn't have to earn.

2. **Tax-Free Money**: This is money for which you pay no taxes when you use it, like qualified distributions from a Roth IRA, a tax-free municipal bond, or a life insurance cash value contract.

3. **Tax-Deferred Money**: This is money that triggers a tax event when you withdraw it, like a traditional IRA, a 401(k) plan, or an annuity (Note: any money you contribute to your 401(k) above your employer's match is tax-deferred money).

4. **Taxable Money**: You're taxed on this money in the year you get it, like your wages or the capital gains you make upon selling an investment.

Free money, of course, is a blessing. If your loved ones have been able to pass along some inheritance money when they die, consider yourself fortunate. If you qualify for a 401(k) with your employer, consider contributing enough to that plan to gain the maximum company match. For example, if your company makes a maximum 3 percent matching contribution (equal to 3 percent of your income), you need to have 3 percent of your earnings withheld from your paycheck for your 401(k). What your company contributes to the plan is free money for you!

There's not much you can do about taxable money. Federal, state and local taxes are going to cut into earnings no matter what. If you sell a stock, mutual fund, real estate or another investment for a profit, you're going to pay taxes on your capital gains.

Next, you'll want to look at strategies that help you balance your tax-free money and tax-deferred money.

Which approach is better—paying taxes on your money now, or paying when you retire and need to use that money?

Well, let me ask you this: if you were a farmer, would you rather pay taxes on the seeds or on your harvest? In which scenario do you think you'll pay more taxes?

Generally, as my clients and seminar audiences respond, you want to pay taxes on those seeds. Of course, that's not always the case. If you save your taxes on a financial product but then overpay in fees, upfront costs, or opportunity costs, you haven't really helped yourself. But most of us would say that, within reason, we would like to pay smaller tax bills in retirement, not larger. And, fortunately, there are a few good ways of doing this:

IRAs, Roth IRAs, and Life Insurance

Three of the most popular retirement savings vehicles today are the 401(k), the traditional IRA (individual retirement account), and the Roth IRA.

As noted, you will probably want to invest enough in your 401(k) to gain the full company match. Any amount of money you invest in the 401(k) plan beyond that is okay, but just understand that all of these funds will be taxed when you take 401(k) distributions upon retirement.

Like the 401(k), the traditional IRA is a tax-deferred retirement instrument. As of 2020, you can contribute a maximum of $6,000 each year to an IRA account if you are under the age of fifty. You pay no taxes when you make that contribution—the taxes come when you take that money out. A tax on the front end reduces your potential earnings, so it's what you might see as an opportunity cost. But a tax on the back end might have more bite because it's reducing the actual money you are able to withdraw.

Let's say your annual income puts you in the 22 percent tax rate bracket. At age forty-nine, you put the maximum $6,000 into an IRA mutual fund. Sure, you didn't have to pay income tax on that money, so you saved about $1,320, and you won't pay taxes on that money as it grows, which allows your money to accumulate even faster — although the taxes will be due someday. Sixteen years later, that money has grown to $15,000 and you're ready to cash it out for your retirement. At a 22 percent rate, you'll pay $3,300 in taxes on that IRA fund. If you happen to need the cash before you reach fifty-nine-and-one-half years old, you'll pay an *additional* 10 percent tax penalty — making it a total of $4,800 in taxes on your $15,000 fund. You just lost nearly a third of your hard-earned IRA money.

A potential alternative is the Roth IRA, which offers tax-free withdrawals. Here's how it works. Let's say you put your $6,000 annual limit into a Roth IRA rather than the traditional IRA. At the front end, you pay your 22 percent tax rate — a total of $1,320 on the $6,000. That's all you pay in taxes. The remaining money can grow tax-free in your Roth IRA account until you need it. Upon retirement, you can withdraw that Roth IRA money without paying any additional taxes. You won't pay taxes on the growth at all.

With the Roth IRA, you are taxing the seed, not the harvest.

Investing in a Roth can be smart for another reason. Many financial professionals, including me, believe that taxes — and tax rates — are going to increase in the future to fund federal programs and pay off the national debt. If you're a young investor, there's also a good chance that you'll advance into a higher tax bracket as you get older and increase your income. Paying a 22 percent tax rate on a Roth IRA investment today, for example, might be more fiscally sound than paying a higher tax rate on the distribution of a traditional IRA when you retire, if taxes do indeed increase in the future. If you need to take your money from a Roth IRA before you turn fifty-nine-and-one-half, you can withdraw your contributions without being subject to taxes or penalties, but any earnings you made on those contributions—any gains you've had in the account—will be subject to the 10 percent federal penalty for early withdrawal.

The Roth IRA can be a great tool, but if your funds are invested in the market, they are subject to the ups and downs of an increasingly volatile stock market. A tax-free municipal bond has lower risk as an investment, but the interest rates tend to be fairly low. It can take a lot of money up-front for a muni bond to effectively balance out the tax penalty. There's another vehicle that offers tax free income that may not come to mind for most people. It's a life insurance contract, and if you need the death benefit it offers, you may want to take a closer look. If you fund it properly, you can build a cash value component within a permanent life insurance contract, which you can use as needed before or during retirement.

The Life Insurance Policy

I often tell my clients that the difference between term and permanent life insurance is like the difference between renting and buying a house. Permanent life insurance is an umbrella term for life insurance policies that do not expire at a set period (although most will mature at an advanced age, usually age 100 or later). Term life insurance, of course, lasts for just a few years depending on the term period you select.

Like renting, term life insurance is less expensive, but you're not building equity. You don't own anything. The premiums for permanent life insurance (also called universal life insurance or cash value life insurance) are typically more expensive. But if you structure the policy and fund it properly, some of the premiums you pay can build cash value that can grow over time, which you may be able to withdraw during your lifetime.[13] And as with all life insurance policies, it provides a death benefit for your beneficiaries when you pass. Also, there are costs and conditions, and you may need to demonstrate that you're healthy through the underwriting process. Your insurance professional can help you select the product that will best fit your needs.

These are great benefits, but the added plus is that these life insurance policies can also help limit your tax exposure.

To accomplish this, we have to get nerdy and look at Section 7702 of the Internal Revenue tax code, which determines how life insurance contracts should be taxed. It's important to understand the maximum amount of money you can pay into a life insurance policy before triggering additional taxation.

Let's say, for example, you've been paying a premium of $100 a month into a cash-value life insurance policy. We'll assume half of that money goes toward the cost of the insurance, and the remaining $50 goes toward the policy's cash value. Then, you learn that, under Section 7702, the IRS allows you to pay a maximum premium of

---

[13] *Policy loans and withdrawals will reduce available cash values and death benefits, and may cause the policy to lapse or affect any guarantees against lapse. Additional premium payments may be required to keep the policy in force. In the event of a lapse, outstanding policy loans in excess of unrecovered cost basis will be subject to ordinary income tax.*

$500 into your policy. You could pay that amount, an additional $450 a month in equity, instead of $50.

Why would you want to do that? Well, for some folks it's because the life insurance policy offers guarantees to your money so that you won't lose value if the market drops. While the value of your Roth IRA will ebb and flow with the whims of the stock market, life insurance contract values are guaranteed by the financial strength of the insurance company issuing them.

Don't Lose the Money Through Taxes!

The bottom line is not everything is doom and gloom about federal debt and taxation. You have some reasonable options for your money that can help improve your tax position after that final paycheck arrives.

By limiting your tax exposure in these vehicles, you can generate additional funds to help supplement your Social Security.

CHAPTER THREE

Family Is Everything

When a potential client visits Fitzwilliams Financial, the first question I ask them is, "What is your goal for retirement?"

Everyone's idea of the ideal retirement is different. It's important for me to learn how they envision their life after work, and what they expect to gain from our services.

Once I have a feel for a person's or a couple's retirement goals, my next question is, "How is your health?"

That might seem like a very personal question to ask a complete stranger right off the bat, but it's a critical one.

From my experience, both personally and professionally, health is the number one factor that can change any financial situation. As I often tell people, "health is wealth." As you get older, the health condition of you and your spouse will have the greatest impact on the quality of your retirement, how much money you can leave for your children, and how many years of "the good life" you can expect once you leave the workforce.

Sometimes, being a financial professional means delivering tough but necessary news. There have been several instances when a client has shared with me a test in which their blood levels are "off," and I've strongly advised them to go see a medical professional right away. I've had clients who have battled cancer, AIDS, and numerous other diseases, and I've worked with all of them on adjusting their retirement income strategies to help address the costs of their medical care.

A few years ago, I had an older client who was experiencing kidney failure, and would have to go into dialysis on a weekly basis soon.

This client's dream vacation had always been to go on a luxury cruise, but she never took the time during her career to take that vacation. We suggested she consider going on that cruise now before she went on dialysis, because she may not be able to go on a cruise again.

The client agreed, had the time of her life on the cruise ship, and then returned to start her dialysis regimen. She later told me she was grateful to have taken the trip when she could fully enjoy it.

Situations like that one are nobody's idea of a dream retirement, but health issues are a reality.

When I ask the people I meet how their health is, most of them answer openly and honestly. They're old enough to understand the gravity of my question, and often have a family member or a friend whose life has been upended by a health scare. By the time they're coming to see me, they understand the value and importance of good health.

Of course, I know the effect poor health can have on a family, starting with my father and mother. I have friends whose careers and livelihoods were stopped in their tracks due to a sickness in the family. Women, especially, seem to have a willingness to walk away from a good income to take care of someone they love.

Through all my years in business, and the thousands of people I've talked with, I've learned that the number one fear of many people age sixty-five and older is running out of money during their retirement. And nothing depletes a person's savings faster than treating a serious health condition without proper preparation.

Health, and the impact it can have on a person and their family, is something I take very seriously.

A Family Approach

At Fitzwilliams Financial, we like to say we treat each other, and our clients, like family.

That may sound cheesy, but it's true. Since starting our company in 2008, my wife Corrine and I have brought on agents, advisors, and other professionals who have the same passion for helping others that we do. When we take on a new client, it's with the idea that we, as a team, are going to be there every single step of the way for the rest of their life.

All of us at Fitzwilliams Financial understand the importance of protecting your savings when challenges arise. Deanna Jones, our chief of operations, learned in 2014 of her father's Stage 4 cancer diagnosis. There was little the doctors could do, and he passed away two months after the diagnosis. Because she was informed, Deanna was able to protect her father's retirement savings, and will be able to pass that money on to her children.

Personally, I wish my parents had someone in their lives like that, someone who was there for them when cancer and heart disease struck, and was able to make the necessary adjustments along the way to help protect their lifestyle.

It was this desire to help that drove me to start Fitzwilliams Financial with a $5,000 investment in 2008.

But launching a company—and keeping it in business—takes a lot more than desire. Fortunately, there were key people who instilled values in me that I hold dear today. Those people gave me the support, skills, and determination that has helped Fitzwilliams Financial grow and prosper for more than decade.

Value, Order, and Persistence

Of course, my parents have had a profound impact on my life.

My mother, Lynnell, taught me the importance of relating to people. She was an outstanding salesperson for our family business for one simple reason: people liked and trusted her.

I would accompany my mom on sales calls and watch how effectively she interacted with prospects. She was a master at finding common ground with people, listening to them, understanding their issues and concerns, and coming up with solutions. My mom understood, as an experienced sales person, that the stronger the connection, the deeper the relationship. Even more than that, she cared about and valued the customers she served.

Today, when I meet potential clients in our seminars or at my office, I always remember my mother's lesson about listening to people and putting their needs first. Helping clients and building relationships is what Fitzwilliams Financial is all about, just as it was for my parents' business, JLT Associates.

My father, who passed away in 2019, had a heart condition during the last thirty-three years of his life. His illness limited some of his time and activities with me when I was young, but it did not limit the profound influence he had on my life.

John Fitzwilliams was a military man. A decorated veteran of the Korean and Vietnam wars, he served in the U.S. Army for twenty-three years, retiring from it before I was born. Later, he owned a jewelry brokerage, Alpha Gem, that served military exchanges globally.

Systems were a part of my father's life, from the military orders he followed to the businesses he created. Process, value, and persistence were his core values, which he poured into me in lesson after lesson throughout my childhood.

He would say, "Timmy, never force things with strength. Use your mind and figure out the easier way to accomplish your goal." From opening a bag of candy to putting together model airplanes, this careful approach always held true with my father.

There's always a right and a wrong way of doing things, he would tell me. I learned this the hard way when I used to clean his car for rewards like sleepovers with friends. Often, I cleaned the car with half-hearted effort and poor results. Dad would explain to me, ever so patiently, what I did wrong.

At the time, I would get mad. But Dad was right. There truly is a right and wrong way to do things. Slowly, I learned to take pride in my work, no matter what it was. I learned to never give up, and that I got what I had earned. If I did a poor job, I earned poor results.

Today, I'm a systems-oriented guy, just like Dad. Everything I do in life has a system, right down to where I leave my shoes, watch, and sunglasses when I come home at night. Everything needs to be organized and in its own little place. I need a system, or I'll screw things up.

My father used to keep a spiral notebook where he logged everything about his business.

I remember walking in and having to be quiet because he was on a sales call. He would tell me, "Timmy, you have to be quiet because if they answer, I only have one shot." So I would sit down next to him and watch him go. He would never stop trying even when told no. This wasn't a simple sales call. He was calling manufacturers asking for the owner so he could represent them to the military.

One day, he got one on the line. We both got so excited. I remember hearing the guy say, "Why do I need you?" Dad clearly and calmly stood his ground and explained how he would make them money. That particular day, he won. He got the deal and picked up a line of crystal: "Never give up Timmy."

When I left for college, my father made it clear to me: I had one chance. We went to McDonald's for breakfast that morning. He introduced me to Paul, the "owner" of the franchise. When we got back home, we stood at the end of the driveway and he explained. "You get one shot and if you fail, you can go talk to Paul, but you can't come back here." I was scared to death, but I understood.

All throughout my life, my father taught me the importance of value, order, and persistence. Lesson after lesson, all the way up to his death. Even on his death bed, he wouldn't give up. He would try to work out. He'd try to get stronger even when there was no hope. He tried until the very end.

You know, I never really understood those lessons until I applied them in my life as an adult. I believe those lessons shaped me into who I am and how I operate every detail of my life today.

American Hustle

I learned about hard work and attention to detail from my dad, but my desire to own and operate my own business has always come natural to me. I like to tell people that I've never had a W-2 form, and that's pretty much the truth.

I've been an entrepreneur since I was a kid. My first paying gig was handing out flyers for a local pizza parlor when I was eleven or twelve years old. Later, my dad helped me acquire a riding lawn mower, and I started my first business cutting grass. There were other endeavors from middle school through college. As a kid, I was always hustling, always selling something.

While attending George Mason University as an economics major, I sold customized auto parts. This was at the height of the *Fast & Furious* movie craze. My business, Concept Auto Creations, sold everything from custom chrome wheels to aluminum diamond floorplates online, and it did pretty well for a few years after college.

Eventually, people got tired of tricking out their cars with specialized auto parts, and I sold Concept Auto Creations. I was twenty-nine years old and anxious to start a business that addressed a permanent need, and one that would also put my knowledge about the economy to work.

I started Fitzwilliams Financial in 2008 by spending $5,000 on sales leads in Richmond, Virginia.

Around this same time, my car was repossessed and my credit was poor. This was when the importance of knowing how to hustle, and also having a business partner I could trust, really came in handy.

My partner was my girlfriend, Corrine, who would later become my wife. During the first year of Fitzwilliams Financial, Corrine let me use her car as we made the two-hour drive to Richmond three or four times a week, and I would call on prospects. Some nights, we wouldn't get back home until 1 a.m.

While I was in an appointment, talking to a potential customer about Fitzwilliams Financial, Corrine would be in her car with a Starbucks coffee and a blanket over her lap, going through the previous prospect's application on her computer. She would then drive to the next call while I was on the phone with other prospects (you can't sell over the phone and drive at the same time—it's too distracting and dangerous).

On a typical visit to Richmond, I'd get in touch with six to eight people, get four of them to agree to meet with me, and convince two of those four to work with Fitzwilliams Financial. We did this consistently for a year, until we had enough money to move our business from our 1,200-square-foot apartment to an office space. We made our first hire soon after that, and the business has continued to grow ever since. In fact, as of today, Fitzwilliams

Financial has grown to ten times its size since the end our first year in business in 2009.

"Always Take Care of Family"

The story of our first year in business together tells you a lot about Corrine's loyalty and level of commitment. Even though we hadn't yet married, we were family, and the bond was already there. Today, Corrine is marketing director of Fitzwilliams Financial, but she covers a wide variety of roles as she helps make sure our clients receive exceptional service.

One of the main principles of Corrine's life, next to "God is good," is this mantra: "Always take care of family." When my parents could no longer live independently, there was no question that they would move into the "mother-in-law's quarters" at our house. Some spouses might have been hesitant about that, but for Corrine, having my parents close was a no-brainer. It was simply the right thing to do. These days, my mother joins our family for dinner almost every night of the week. And she has company, because Corrine's mother lives at our house, too.

All through my life, I've been blessed to be surrounded by people whose passion and commitment helped make me a better person. Without them, we couldn't have built the team we have at Fitzwilliams Financial—a team dedicated to doing the right thing by helping our clients reach their retirement goals every step of the way.

CHAPTER FOUR

Basic 401(k) Math: "What Percent Is It?"

Do you have a 401(k) plan?

If you do, how is that plan working for you?

You'd be surprised by how many people I speak with who have faithfully invested in a 401(k), but have little idea as to how it is performing.

They can't tell you their 401(k)'s annual rate of return, or how it's performing against the S&P 500 or other stock market indices. They may have poured tens of thousands of dollars in retirement money into in their 401(k)—or into multiple 401(k) plans—but have little awareness as to how well it is meeting their retirement goals.

If you're like many of these folks, you'll look up your 401(k) balance online every couple of months, or maybe you'll glance at the quarterly statement. You'll scan through the numbers, quickly noting that there are more green arrows than red arrows, then stuff the document in a desk drawer. The fund seems to be working okay and, after all, you've got more pressing matters right now than thinking about retirement, which seems so far away.

You're not alone. Americans are notorious for their casual approach to 401(k) plans, if they even think about them at all. That's ironic, since the 401(k) was created, in part, to allow consumers to exercise more control over their retirement funds, as opposed to traditional, employer-controlled pension plans. According to U.S. census data, an estimated 79 percent of Americans work for an employer that offers access to a 401(k) plan. However, only 41 percent of those workers choose to participate. Overall, an estimated 32 percent of the total workforce is saving in a 401(k).[14]

In other words, many American workers are passing up free money from their employers, who typically will match 3 percent or more of a worker's salary if they participate in the plan. And it's not as though investing in a 401(k) is a big hassle. You can set your contribution rate, and have it automatically deducted from your paycheck, along with all those local, state, and federal taxes you have to pay.

Perhaps the ease of socking money away into a 401(k) is one reason many investors seem to treat it like the basement smoke alarm. You know, every year or so you replace the battery in your smoke alarm, and in my experience, that's about how often many people check on the progress of their 401(k)s.

Of course, it's important to have a clear understanding of how much money your 401(k) is making, so you can adjust your holdings and investments in that fund accordingly. And measuring your fund's performance is an incredibly simple calculation—anyone who

---

[14] Maurie Backman. The Motley Fool. June 19, 2017. "Does the Average American Have a 401(k)?" https://www.fool.com/retirement/2017/06/19/does-the-average-american-have-a-401k.aspx

understands common math can do it. I explain how to do it in the following, and share three additional commonsense lessons about 401(k)s.

Do the Math

Want to get a quick idea of what kind of a return you're getting from your 401(k) retirement fund? Here's a quick calculation:

1. Subtract from your 401(k) balance the amount of money you or your employer have contributed to it over the life of the fund.

2. Once you've subtracted your contributions, take the remaining amount and divide it by the number of years you have contributed to the fund.

3. Once you've learned the amount of money your fund is making, on average, each year, divide that number by the amount of money invested into the fund.

4. Now you have an annual rate of return on your fund, but you're not finished yet. Subtract from that rate any annual management fees you pay on the fund. Now you have a ballpark idea of how your 401(k) is performing.

Here's an example of how that works: Let's say you've had a 401(k) plan for twenty-three years. Over that period of time, $250,000 has been invested into the fund by you and your employer. Your fund balance as of today is $500,000.

So, about how much is your 401(k) making? If you subtract your contributions from the fund balance, you're left with $250,000.

Divide that figure by 23—the number of years you've been investing in the 401(k)—and you're earning about $10,869 a year.

Now, what's the percentage rate? Divide that $10,859 by the $250,000 you've put into the fund, and you arrive at a rate of 4.34 percent. Subtract from the 1 percent a year you're paying in management fees, and you've arrived a true rate of return of 3.34 percent each year.

That's just barely beating out the annual rate of inflation.[15] However, compared with the national IRA average rate of return of 2.2 percent, your 401(k) fund is doing pretty well.[16]

Now, this rate of return is simplistic because it treats your investments as though they performed consistently year after year. In reality, there were likely years that the market dropped and you lost money, where your rate of return would actually be something like negative 15 percent. In other years, your rate of return might have been a positive 20 percent. But, this average rate of return is an "easy" way of calculating what your investing looks like if you were able to draw it on a straight line, as opposed to the actual spikes and drops of real-time market performance.

---

[15] US Inflation Calculator. 2020. "Current US Inflation Rates: 2009-2020." https://www.usinflationcalculator.com/inflation/current-inflation-rates/

[16] Robert C. Lawton. *Forbes*. March 3, 2019. "12 Reasons Not to Roll Your 401(k) into an IRA." https://www.forbes.com/sites/robertlawton/2019/03/03/12-reasons-not-to-roll-your-401k-into-an-ira/#f27242b299d7

Don't Let Your 401(k) Just Sit There!

Now that you know how to calculate just how hard your 401(k) is working for you, make a point of doing regular check-ins to make sure you are optimizing your rate of return.

Borrowing Against Your 401(k)

Withdrawing money from your 401(k) before you reach the age of fifty-nine-and-one-half is generally a bad idea, because the taxes and penalties on that withdrawal can be severe.

Still, an amazing number of American workers do exactly that. More than 40 percent of the 15 million 401(k) participants who change jobs in a given year simply cash out their 401(k) instead of rolling it over into an IRA or a new employer's plan.[17]

Here's why this might be a mistake. If you cash out a traditional 401(k), you'll owe income tax on that withdrawal. And if you're younger than fifty-nine-and-one-half when you cash out, you'll owe an additional 10 percent early withdrawal penalty.

So, let's say you're forty years old. You have $50,000 in your 401(k), and you decide to cash it out instead of rolling it into your new employer's plan. Let's assume income tax is 20 percent, which cuts the withdrawal amount to $40,000. Then, the 10 percent penalty

---

[17] Barry Levie Financial. November 20, 2018. "Loans and Cash-Outs: These 401(k) Issues Could Haunt Retirees."
https://www.barryleviefinancial.com/blog/loans-and-cash-outs-these-401k-issues-could-haunt-retirees

cuts your total amount by another $5,000. So now you're down to $35,000. And that doesn't even account for state taxes—many U.S. states will also tax early 401(k) withdrawals.

Even worse than the tax and penalty is the missed opportunity to watch that money grow in your 401(k) through investing and compound interest. Depending on what you do with your money after you've withdrawn it, your funds may be failing to keep up with the possible rate of inflation.

Do You Have a 401(k) Collection?

In today's mobile workforce, some people pile up old 401(k) plans the way other people collect comic books or vinyl records.

These workers move from one employer to the next over the years, and never bother to do anything with the 401(k) money they leave behind. The old plans sit in the old company's plan. How much of an annual return are these plans generating? Their owners probably don't have the faintest idea unless they're paying attention to the annual statements they get.

Many of today's workers are going to have a number of different employers during their lifetimes. Long gone are the days when you could count on a steady, thirty-five-year career with the same company, building up a nice pension along the way. According to the Bureau of Labor Statistics, the average U.S. worker holds a total of ten different jobs by the age of forty.[18] Data from Gallup show that millennials—and likely generations who come after—are more likely than generations before them to job hop.[19]

That means you'll likely be toiling for a lot of different employers—and investing in a number of different 401(k) plans—throughout your career.

When you start a new job for a new company, sometimes the last thing on your mind is the money sitting in your previous employer's 401(k). Figuring out what to do with that money can be kind of a hassle, especially when you have more immediate concerns with your new paying gig.

Once you have settled into your new job, you will likely want to take action on that old 401(k). You have a few options: you could cash it out, you could roll the money into an IRA or Roth IRA retirement fund (which you or a financial advisor could manage), or you could roll it into your new employer's 401(k).

There are a few things to keep in mind when you're thinking about a rollover. Of course, I'm not licensed to provide specific investment advice, but there are a few generalities that we should all think about when we have the opportunity in front of us.

---

[18] Bureau of Labor Statistics. August 22, 2019. "Number of Jobs, Labor Market Experience, and Earnings Growth: Results From a National Longitudinal Survey." https://www.bls.gov/news.release/pdf/nlsoy.pdf

[19] Amy Adkins. Gallup Business Journal. 2017. Millennials: The Job-Hopping Generation." https://www.gallup.com/workplace/231587/millennials-job-hopping-generation.aspx

- Rolling over that 401(k) into a new fund you can continue investing in gives you more control over the money than allowing it to sit in an old portfolio of funds.

- Often, a 401(k) rollover is as simple as making a phone call to the fund manager. Be sure to have accurate information on which retirement account you want the money rolled into. The manager of the old 401(k) will then cut a check to the fund manager of the new plan or IRA, and the money will go into that account within a few days. It's a simple transaction.

- When changing jobs, if you let more than six months go by before finding a new home for your old 401(k) money, you may not get around to doing something with that old fund until several years—and jobs—later.

- Know what your old company's policy is—some plans have a policy of automatically rolling that 401(k) into an IRA at the same company (often with a fee for doing so) or of sending you a check, which should give you an extra incentive to take action on your old 401(k) to avoid any unnecessary fees or taxes.

- Think twice before you opt not to do a rollover of any kind and instead cash out the account. Employers cutting a lump-sum check to you from your retirement accounts are required to take 20 percent off the top for federal income taxes, and it still may not be enough to cover what you'll owe come tax time. This is because distributions from tax-deferred retirement plans are subject to federal income tax and may likely also be subject to a 10 percent federal tax penalty if you cash those funds out before age fifty-nine-and-one-half. This makes it very important to consider your rollover options before just asking for a check.

When used correctly, the 401(k) plan can be an effective instrument for retirement savings.

So, be better than the average investor. Don't neglect your 401(k).

CHAPTER FIVE

Social Security: When Should You Take It?

S ocial Security might be at risk for today's younger workers. But for those who are anticipating retirement in the next few years, Social Security will be a significant part of their income once they leave the workforce.

Which begs the question I get all the time from clients and prospects: At what age should I start collecting my Social Security?

The standard answer is that, if you take Social Security at the earliest eligible age, sixty-two, you'll get 73.3 percent of the monthly benefit, because you took it fifty-two months early. If you start collecting on Social Security at sixty-five, you'll receive 91 percent of the monthly benefit. If you wait until sixty-six, you'll reap 100 percent of your monthly Social Security benefit.

So, waiting longer means getting more money each month? Yes, but it's not quite that cut and dry when it comes to timing your collection.

There's a story I like to tell in these situations.

Once upon a time, there lived three brothers: Earl, Stan, and Del.

These brothers happened to be triplets, and all three of them worked the same kind of job for the exact same amount of money. But these three brothers had different ideas of when they wanted to retire and start collecting Social Security. Earl wanted to take it early, at age sixty-two, so he could start banking the Social Security checks and earn interest on them. Stan wanted to wait until the standard retirement age, at sixty-six. And Del wanted to maximize his income by delaying Social Security for as long as he could, and not start collecting until age seventy.

So, which brother has the right approach to timing his Social Security? The answer is that all of them could be correct, or they could all be wrong. Because the right time to collect on Social Security depends on your individual health, your personal values and, of course, the economy and other circumstances beyond your control.

Like interest rates, for example. If Earl can get a great interest rate—say, 7 percent or so—by investing his Social Security money, then it might make sense that he would not want to wait until age sixty-six. He could start putting that money away now and earning money off of his invested Social Security benefits.

Mortality is a big factor. For Del to maximize his Social Security income by delaying until seventy, he'll have to live past eighty-seven to reap the full benefits. That might be a smart move if Del is in excellent health with a strong family history of longevity. However, if Del's a lifelong smoker, has survived a bout or two with cancer, or underwent major heart surgery in his younger years, he might be better off collecting Social Security earlier.

Understanding your health and having a realistic expectation of your mortality should inform your decision about when the right age is for you to collect Social Security.

Human behavior is another factor. When I discuss Social Security during my seminar, I note that most of the women in the room are going to agree with me within ten seconds after making the following statement: No matter how much a woman makes, what her education is, or what professional title she holds, she will give it all up at the drop of a hat for someone, or something, she cares about. And all the women in the audience nod in agreement.

I have a client who was a director of human resources for the government up north. She was awarded a large promotion, but she had to retire early to care for her youngest daughter, who was stricken with brain cancer. She's now the most qualified underpaid HR director currently residing along the oceanfront of Virginia Beach, but she hasn't given it a second thought. Walking away from a successful career and six-figure income to help her daughter was an easy decision.

Deciding when to take Social Security may also be dictated by the unexpected. You know the old joke about the easiest way to make God laugh? Have a plan.

What if your life heading into retirement was perfect, but your children's lives weren't so great? A growing social change in America is the number of retirees who are becoming parents again—to their grandchildren. That's not something you may plan for or have budgeted to do, but it could happen. The probability of kids growing up in "grand families" has more than doubled since 1970.[20] According to the Centers for Disease Control, some 2.6 million grandparents are raising their grandchildren today, due to factors affecting the parents including everything from military deployment to drug abuse to untimely death.[21]

In the case of an unexpected event like caring for your grandchildren, taking out Social Security a little earlier than expected could provide a much-needed financial cushion for you and your family during retirement.

The lesson of Earl, Stan, and Del is that, when it comes to collecting on Social Security, there's no one-size-fits-all answer. Everyone's life is unique, and everyone has different financial goals.

Deciding when the time is right for you to take Social Security depends on more than just your financial condition, or how long you plan to continue to work. A thorough self-evaluation of your health, your family, and what might transpire a few years down the road, should also factor into your decision on when to start using the social safety net.

---

[20] Renee R. Ellis and Tavia Simmons. Census.gov. October 2014. "Coresident Grandparents and Their Grandchildren."
https://www.census.gov/content/dam/Census/library/publications/2014/demo/p20-576.pdf

[21] Robin Marantz Henig. The Atlantic. June 1, 2018. "The Age of Grandparents Is Made of Many Tragedies."
https://www.theatlantic.com/family/archive/2018/06/this-is-the-age-of-grandparents/561527/

CHAPTER SIX

Social Security and Taxation

There's a game I like to play with my seminar audiences that's about Social Security and retirement.

The game is called, "Pay Your Taxes."

Trust me—it's a little more fun than it sounds.

I divide the room into two groups, and I start handing out bags of money. Each person in the first group gets $2. Each person in the second group gets $3. Sometimes I'll split the room by gender and give the women $2 each. Am I short-changing the ladies? We'll have to wait and see.

Here's how the game is played: The members of the $2 group each have that money invested in a tax-deferred product, like an IRA. Those who are in the $3 group have their money in a five-year bank CD.

Clearly, the people with $3 are better off than those who only have $2, right?

Well, maybe not.

It's tax time. Let's start with the $3 group—the $3 they hold in their bags is the interest they've earned on their bank CDs—it's directly reportable income. Also, it's important to note that each of these folks is at the $34,000 level, filing jointly, for household income for the purpose of this exercise.

What that means is that 18 percent of the $3 they've earned goes to taxes. Federal taxes in this case would be 12 percent, and, since we're in Virginia, nearly 6 percent in state income taxes.

That takes 36 cents from the $3 in earnings, for a net gain of $2.64. Not too bad, and still more than the $2 from the other group.

But, *wait*! Don't forget Social Security taxes!

A lot of people forget that, even though you paid for your Social Security benefit through payroll taxes during your working years, you may still have to pay taxes on the benefits you receive once you retire. The federal government taxes a percentage of Social Security benefits based on what they call your "combined" income. Combined income means half of your Social Security benefits plus your other income, including interest earned on other sources that isn't otherwise taxable. In layman's terms, this means the interest payment you earned on that tax-free municipal bond could still make your Social Security benefits taxable.

So, to review:

Your regular taxable income (adjusted gross income)
+ ½ of your annual Social Security benefit
+ any additional untaxed interest earnings
———————————————————————
= combined income

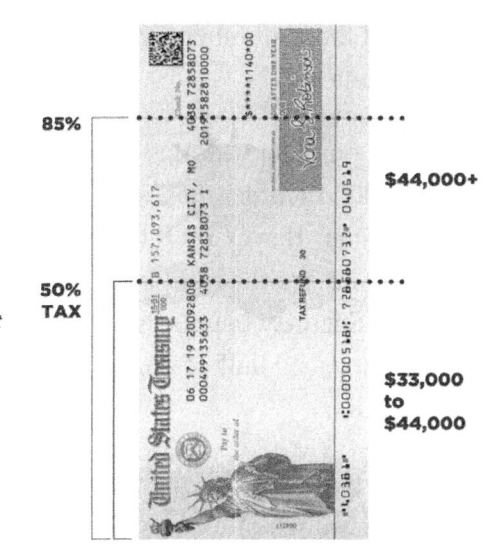

Check is included as an example and doesn't represent the specific Social Security situation of any particular individual.

Depending on your combined income, you may have to pay taxes on 50 or 85 percent of your benefits. The following chart shows a quick calculation of how much of your benefits will be taxable depending on your filing status and income.

Social Security Taxation		
% of SS Subject to Tax	Single Filer with Combined Income___	Married Filing Jointly with Combined Income ___
0%	<$25,000	<$32,000
50%	$25,000-$34,000	$32,000-$44,000
85%	$34,000+	$44,000+

If you look at those numbers, you'll see there isn't too much wiggle room in these taxes.

To return to our lucky dollar folks, let's say, in addition to their regular $34,000 income, they also make $20,000 annually in Social Security income. If we add half of that, or $10,000, to our regular $34,000 income, we toe right up to the $44,000 line where only half of the Social Security benefit is subject to income tax. If we have to pay income taxes on half of our Social Security, we're looking at an $1,800 tax bill.

Oh, but with that extra $3, the members of this group now each has a combined earnings of exactly $44,003.

That means that *85 percent* of their Social Security benefit is taxable, in addition to the 36 cents in income tax they are paying on that $3!

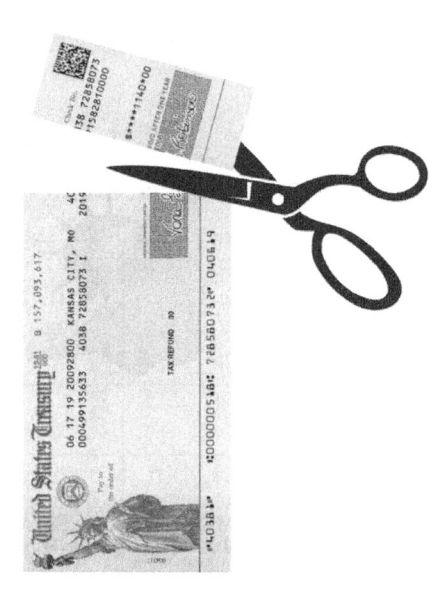

If 85 percent of Social Security is taxable, that means paying $3,060 in income taxes on Social Security benefits. Thanks to the extra $3, the people in that group got the privilege of paying <u>an extra $1,260.36</u> in taxes. Who would have thought a measly $3 could have made such a difference—more than $1,000—in a person's tax bill?

Still think the $3 group has the advantage?

What about the people who only received $2 in my little game? Well, each of those people invested that $2 in an IRA, which is a tax-deferred retirement plan. That means no annual tax while the money remains in the IRA, gaining interest on a tax-deferred basis. Now, they will at some point have to pay income tax on those benefits. But in the meantime, they can develop a plan for how to strategically make their withdrawals in a way that most benefits them and maybe avoids triggering those higher taxes.

And, for today, they get to keep their $2 without having to pay out extra taxes on their Social Security benefits! Most people don't realize the difference each dollar can make when it comes to issues like Social Security taxation. This is something that concerns me a lot. There's a story in our industry about a retired client who wanted to upgrade his backyard. The cost of the improvements was about $70,000, so this client took $100,000 out of his 401(k).

That withdrawal meant his income was well over the $44,000 threshold that particular year, so he was one of those unfortunate people whose onetime withdrawal drastically affected not only his regular income taxes, but also the taxes due on his Social Security benefits for the year.

The lesson behind the "Pay Your Taxes" game is that a simple rule from the IRS can make retirement a lot more complicated than you might imagine. Whether you're retired or not, the impact of Social Security taxes is something you should keep in mind. And, if you're still working, Social Security tax isn't something your accountant tallies since it's automatically deducted from your paycheck. This is another reason I think everyone should be sure they're working not just with some maverick financial professional, but with a professional who has a team and works in coordination to cover all of their bases. You want everyone pulling in the same direction and cross communicating so little things—like $3 extra dollars—don't cause bigger-dollar issues.

Just remember the $44,000 income cap and the consequences of exposing too much of your retirement income to taxation. It's cold comfort, I know. But this awareness can inspire more effective, disciplined retirement planning once you understand all of the possible scenarios.

As I like to tell my clients, "If you have a hole in your boat, you'll want to fix that hole quickly, even if it's above the water line. Don't wait until the boat is weighed down and sinking to worry about holes."

Which brings me to another little tidbit about Social Security that a lot of folks don't know about, and something most married couples don't even want to think about . . .

CHAPTER SEVEN

The "Transfer on Death" Trap

Most of us don't want to dwell too much on what life would be like without our spouse. That's our rock, our partner in life—the loving person who co-raised the kids, lived through job losses and promotions, endured our parents, and still doesn't gripe too much when we pull the sheets over to our side of the bed. This is the person we want to retire and enjoy the "golden years" with.

Sadly, retirement doesn't always play out that way. When a husband or wife dies, there are many harsh, unpleasant decisions for the surviving spouse to make. Transferring retirement accounts, life insurance, investments, and personal property can be made much easier if you and your spouse have a will and trust.

But there's also the question of what to do with your spouse's Social Security benefits. As with many things having to do with Social Security, the answer seems simple, but it can severely complicate your life once you really think about it.

I call it the "Transferal in Death" Trap.

Here's what happens when a person who has Social Security benefits dies and leaves behind a surviving spouse or child: Social Security pays out to the survivor a lump-sum death benefit of $255.

That benefit can also be broken into smaller monthly payments called a survivor benefit.

The surviving spouse can also collect the late spouse's Social Security benefit once the survivor has reached retirement age (that's sixty-six if you were born before 1954, and sixty-seven if you were born in 1960 or later).

However, the survivor cannot collect their own Social Security benefit along with that of their deceased spouse. Social Security will pay out the higher of the two amounts.

That sounds fair, doesn't it? Even generous, perhaps.

That is, until you apply this scenario to your standard of living.

Here's an example: Claire and Frank have been happily married for thirty-five years, and are just starting to enjoy their retirement. They are both sixty-eight and collecting Social Security benefits. Frank collects $3,000 a month from Social Security, while Claire collects $2,000.

Sadly, Frank collapses of a heart attack on the golf course, leaving Claire all of his assets, including a cherry red 1965 Mustang convertible and his prized collection of Beach Boys vinyl records.

Since she is the surviving spouse, Claire starts collecting Frank's $3,000 monthly Social Security check because it's the larger amount. But that means she has to give up her $2,000 monthly check.

As an individual, Claire is now collecting more from Social Security. But her monthly household income from Social Security has decreased from $5,000 to $3,000 since Frank's death. Overall, it's a net loss for Claire and a penalty for losing her spouse. She may even have to sell Frank's '65 Mustang to help bridge the gap.

One other thing of note: Remember how I mentioned that Frank and Claire were both sixty-eight years old? Let's say Frank started collecting Social Security at age sixty-two, before reaching his full retirement age. According to the Social Security scale, that means Claire can only collect 81 percent of her husband's Social Security benefit, since he decided to start taking it early.

What can be done about this less-than-ideal scenario? Not a darn thing until and unless Social Security changes this (don't hold your breath on that one).

My purpose in sharing this story is not to bum you out. It's to illustrate the importance of planning for retirement and anticipating some of the financial pitfalls. Hopefully, you won't have to worry about the loss of your husband or wife until both of you are at very advanced ages. However, if a sad event like the untimely loss of a spouse does happen, you'll have at least prepared for the potential loss of some of your family's Social Security income.

Other Things to Keep In Mind

There are some other important Social Security rules to keep in mind in determining if you would qualify for survivor benefits.

• Typically, you have to wait until full retirement age to start receiving your spouse's benefits. However, if you are disabled you can start collecting at age fifty. If you are caring for a child who is disabled or under the age of sixteen, you can collect 75 percent of your late spouse's benefit, regardless of your age.

• If you are below full retirement age and still working, your survivor benefit could be affected by Social Security's earnings limit.

• Even if you divorced your late spouse, you could still qualify for survivor benefits based on his or her work record.

• If you claim survivor benefits between age sixty and your full retirement age, your portion of the deceased's benefit will range between 71.5 percent and 99 percent, depending how close you are to the full retirement age.

• If you happen to hear wedding bells again, it may pay off to wait a while. If the next marriage takes place before you turn sixty, you cannot draw survivor benefits from your late spouse. However, if you re-marry after sixty, you're still eligible for survivor benefits (you can even regain the benefits if your next marriage ends).

Again, the transferal in death of Social Security benefits is not a pleasant thing to think about or discuss. That's probably why many people avoid the topic completely.

In my discussions with potential clients, most of them can't explain what will happen to their Social Security if their husband or wife dies. Some of them are even surprised to hear they are entitled to their late spouse's benefits.

My advice to anyone dealing with the loss of a spouse is to be proactive and get in touch with the Social Security office right away.

Your spouse's benefits—if they do happen to be more than your own—will only start after you apply for them.

If you're like Claire and already retired, you might find yourself facing a hit to your household income. However, collecting the greater of the two Social Security benefits is something that you, as the survivor, are entitled to and they will be paid out for the rest of your life.

That's assuming, of course, that Social Security will still be there when you retire.

CHAPTER EIGHT

The Trouble with Required Minimum Distributions

If you're approaching retirement, you've probably had someone tell you about required minimum distributions—"RMDs" for short. Chances are the person who told you about them didn't have too many nice things to say about RMDs. No one outside of the Internal Revenue Service seems to particularly like them.

So you may have heard a thing or two about RMDs from your parents, or perhaps from that older gentleman who corners you every year at the neighborhood holiday cocktail party. But do you really know what RMDs are, and how they can affect your retirement income?

Basically, required minimum distributions are mandatory withdrawals you have to take each year out of tax-deferred retirement funds like a traditional IRA or 401(k). Until President Donald Trump signed the Secure Act retirement system reform in 2019, you had to start taking RMDs from your IRAs at seventy-and-one-half years old. Now, thanks to the new law, you can wait until you are seventy-two. For 401(k)s, the withdrawal begins either when you fully retire or at seventy-and-one-half, whichever comes first.

The amount you are required to withdraw changes each year. The IRS has a table of divisors it uses to calculate your annual RMD, which is based on your age and the average person's life expectancy.

It's your responsibility to use this formula every year to determine your RMD and then withdraw that amount each year. Your first RMD must be taken by April 1 following the calendar year you turn seventy-two (if you choose to wait until then). For each of the following years, you will have until December 31 to make the withdrawal.

Here is an example of how an RMD works. Henry has $100,000 in a traditional IRA. Last year, he turned seventy-and-one-half, and he has chosen to take out his first RMD by April 1 of this year. Henry goes on Google and quickly finds the IRS required minimum distribution table, which informs him that he has a "distribution period" of 27.4 for his age.

Here's what Henry does with that information:

1. He looks up his IRA balance from December 31 of the previous year, which is $100,000.

2. He divides that balance by 27.4, and arrives at $3,649.63.

3. That $3,649.63 is Henry's RMD for that year, the amount he must withdraw before April 1.

Sounds pretty simple, right? But here's where things get complicated: That divisor for Henry's RMD changes each year after seventy-and-one-half. As Henry gets older, the divisor becomes smaller, which means the amount Henry has to withdraw each year gets larger. At age eighty, he'll have to divide his IRA holdings by

18.7. If Henry lives to be ninety, he'll divide his balance by 11.4. And so on, until Henry dies.

And if Henry *miscalculates* his RMD and doesn't withdraw enough money, the tax penalty can be stiff. He may face a tax rate of up to 50 percent on the RMD money he failed to take out.

Below is an image of the official RMD table from the IRS, just in case you're curious about how it plays out—all the way up to 115 years old and beyond!

Required Minimum Distributions							
Age	Distribution Period	Age	Distribution Period	Age	Distribution Period	Age	Distribution Period
70	27.4	82	17.1	94	9.1	106	4.2
71	26.5	83	16.3	95	8.6	107	3.9
72	25.6	84	15.5	96	8.1	108	3.7
73	24.7	85	14.8	97	7.6	109	3.4
74	23.8	86	14.1	98	7.1	110	3.1
75	22.9	87	13.4	99	6.7	111	2.9
76	22.0	88	12.7	100	6.3	112	2.6
77	21.2	89	12.0	101	5.9	113	2.4
78	20.3	90	11.4	102	5.5	114	2.1
79	19.5	91	10.8	103	5.2	115+	1.9
80	18.7	92	10.2	104	4.9		
81	17.9	93	9.6	105	4.5		

Source: Internal Revenue Service

Managing Your RMDs

Why does the government mandate that you withdraw a certain amount of money from your IRA or 401(k) each year?

You probably know the answer to that question. Because IRAs and 401(k)s are tax-deferred retirement accounts, they are not subject to taxation until you make withdrawals. The RMDs are an opportunity for the IRS to generate tax revenue from your retirement funds.

It's important to note that RMD withdrawals are typically taxed as ordinary income. That means they will count toward your total taxable income for the year, and will be taxed at your individual federal income tax rate. In some cases, local and state taxes may also take a cut out of your RMDs.

If you have multiple IRAs and 401(k) funds, as many retirees do, it's important to know that you do not have to take a distribution from each one of those accounts.

Getting back to our friend Henry's example for a moment—each year, he receives a letter from each one of his retirement fund managers informing him of the exact dollar amount to withdraw from each of those accounts to satisfy his RMD. However, the fund managers for Henry's IRAs and 401(k) are probably not talking to each other. They're likely unaware of how much money Henry has in all of his tax-deferred retirement accounts.

Henry should know, though. So it's up to him (or his financial advisor) to add up those funds as of December 31 of the previous year and calculate the RMD. From there, Henry has some flexibility. He can take the RMD out of just one account, or from multiple accounts. As long as he withdraws the correct amount of money, the particular funds he takes it from do not matter to the IRS.

One approach Henry could take is to have a "burn account" for his RMDs. In other words, instead of taking the RMD money out of an IRA or 401(k) that's generating a healthy return, why not use a retirement account that's underperforming? Maybe there's an IRA that Henry opened in 1992 that's heavy on bonds and has a long-in-the-tooth mutual fund? It's generating a paltry 3 percent average annual return, but there's more than $20,000 in it. That IRA could be Henry's burn account to address RMDs for the next few years.

It's also important to note that Henry has a full year to decide when to exercise his RMD. He might want to let his retirement money grow for several months before taking a distribution late in the year. Or perhaps Henry wants to use the money to meet expenses, so it might be best to take the RMD earlier.

Taking your RMD withdrawal in smaller, scheduled amounts—instead of in one lump sum—is also an option, with some help from a financial professional or an advisor. You can always elect to have your taxes withheld from your RMD when you take the distribution. If you don't, be sure to set aside the right amount of money for taxes, so as to avoid any unpleasant surprises come next April 15.

What to Do With RMD Money?

So you've taken your RMD distribution, as required by the federal government. You've had the taxes withheld. What do you do with the cash that remains?

The short answer is you can do anything you want with it. If you're able to live off your pension, Social Security, or other savings, and you don't need the RMD distribution to meet expenses, here are some ideas on where to put that money:

• **Non-retirement investments:** You can always put the money right back into the market, just not into another tax-advantaged retirement account. Tax-free municipal bonds, exchange-traded funds, tax-managed mutual funds, or stocks that you plan to hang onto for more than a year are some effective ways to reinvest and also limit your tax exposure.

• **Charity:** If you need to take an RMD but also plan on giving to a worthy cause, you can accomplish both by opening a Qualified Charitable Distribution (QCD). A QCD is a direct transfer of funds from the manager of your IRA fund to a qualified charity. The QCD amount counts toward your RMD distribution for the year, with an annual maximum of $100,000.

• **Inheritance:** Your RMD withdrawals might be a nice way to build a little fund your grandkids can use when they get older. You could put the money into a 529 college savings plan, a trust fund or a Roth IRA for Kids account. You could also convert one of your IRAs into a Roth IRA, using your RMD money to pay the taxes that go along with the conversion. Upon death, your children—or grandchildren—will inherit their share of the Roth IRA tax-free.

There's also life insurance. If you want to avoid hurting your beneficiaries' inheritance by raiding their trust funds, you might consider buying life insurance, if you're healthy enough to qualify for it. The death benefit from that life insurance will be tax-free, and generally should be much more than what you spent on premiums.

What If You Need the Money Now?

You may have immediate use for money you withdraw in an RMD, which make sense. Your IRA and 401(k) are, after all, designed to help fund your retirement.

If you do rely on RMDs to help pay for expenses, it's important to maintain a retirement budget and have clear visibility as to how much you expect to take in withdrawals each year. You'll also need a plan for what you'll spend that money on, and how it can help with your cash flow. Putting the RMD money into a bank account that offers cash management tools could help you maximize how you cover your retirement expenses.

One thing to remember: The RMD is *not* intended as some sort of guide on how much money you should be withdrawing from your tax-deferred retirement accounts every year. The RMD is solely intended to generate more tax revenue for the IRS. You enjoyed the benefit of a tax deduction in the year you made the contribution and didn't have to pay taxes while it was growing, so now it's time to pay those taxes to the IRS.

So don't make the mistake of believing you should limit yourself to whatever money you pull out for the RMD, particularly since the total amount could differ greatly from one year of your retirement to the next. Take the RMD total into account when you determine how much in withdrawals you need to make to help meet your retirement expenses. A full understanding of your total savings and costs should direct your decision on how much money to take out.

CHAPTER NINE

Long-Term Care: It Could Happen to You

It will happen when you least expect it.

I just helped a seventy-four-year-old client transfer assets who was, until recently, the picture of health. He was in good physical shape and, as former teacher, his mind was sharp as a tack.

Recently, on a hot summer afternoon, my client was mowing his yard when his legs suddenly gave way. He lay in the grass, unable to get up, for six hours, suffering a heat stroke in the process. Today, he's in a wheelchair, with much of his mental facilities gone. He's in a long-term care state, likely for the rest of his life.

And that's how it happens.

In an instant, you can go from feeling healthy and happy to an uncertain future of chronic pain and nursing care. It doesn't have to be something dramatic. It can happen when you slip in the bathroom, or if you trip on an uneven seam in the sidewalk.

The elderly are most vulnerable. As I mentioned before, my dad had his health problems in the later years of his life. But he was always active and physically fit. He was eighty years old and still doing pull-ups. Pull-ups at eighty!

One day, while trying to balance a hot coffee with a sack of food while opening his front door, he tripped and fell into the bushes, cracking several ribs.

Dad never recovered. He was in long-term care for the rest of his life.

The Costs of Long-Term Care

For many families, long-term care is a significant financial challenge. The expense is a national concern that seems to be only getting worse, and the toll it takes on the patient as well as his or her caregivers can be tremendous. Many retirees I speak with aren't afraid of dying. They're terrified of someday needing assistance for basic daily activities like eating, bathing, and going to the bathroom. Not just for a few days or weeks, but for several months, and likely for the rest of their lives. Not only is this a miserable way to live, the costs of hospital or in-home care can quickly deplete their retirement savings, as well as the savings of their children.

A recent survey from the Nationwide Retirement Institute found that more than 70 percent of respondents age fifty and above listed out-of-control health care costs as their greatest fear.[22] In one Nationwide Retirement Institute survey, roughly half of those

---

[22] Nationwide Retirement Institute, as seen on PRNewswire. June 26, 2018. "Even affluent Americans are concerned about health care costs and their impact on retirement plans." https://www.prnewswire.com/news-releases/even-affluent-americans-are-concerned-about-health-care-costs-and-their-impact-on-retirement-plans-300672245.html

surveyed said they would rather die than end up in nursing home care.²³

Genworth Financial has a useful online calculator that estimates the cost of different levels of long-term care by geographic region at https://www.genworth.com/aging-and-you/finances/cost-of-care.html. The numbers aren't pretty, no matter where you live. According to Genworth, this was the national average *monthly* cost of care in 2019:

    Homemaker Services: $4,290

    Home Health Aid: $4,385

    Assisted Living Facility: $4,051

    Nursing Home Semi-Private Room: $7,513

    Nursing Home Private Room: $8,517

Of course, the costs of care are rising all the time. According to a recent Genworth survey, the annual median cost of a private nursing home room rose 1.82 percent in 2019, to $102,200. The cost of a home health aide increased 4.55 percent, to $52,624 a year.²⁴

---

²³ Darla Mercado. CNBC Markets. October 30, 2019. "More than half of adults over 50 would rather die than do this." https://www.cnbc.com/2019/10/30/more-than-half-of-adults-over-50-would-rather-die-than-do-this.html

²⁴ Genworth Financial. October 16, 2019. "Genworth Cost of Care Survey 2019: Skyrocketing care costs may make the dream of aging at home more challenging." http://investor.genworth.com/investors/news-releases/archive/archive/2019/Genworth-Cost-of-Care-Survey-2019-Skyrocketing-care-costs-may-make-the-dream-of-aging-at-home-more-challenging/default.aspx

Do I have your attention yet? I know—it's eye-opening.

An excellent 2018 series of columns by *Washington Post* personal finance writer Michelle Singletary examined long-term care. She reported that, as the cost of medical care rises and many Americans live into their nineties, little has been done to address the cost of providing care for those people who can no longer take care of themselves. One reader responded to her columns with a story about how the expense of long-term care for her father made her stressed out and even resentful.

"Every day he was living was costing me so much money that I wished he would die already," the reader wrote. "And that's a horrible thing to think."

What about government assistance? Well, Medicare doesn't cover long-term care. Medicaid does provide coverage, but you have to be pretty poor—owning less than $2,000 in assets other than your house) to receive that benefit. The Affordable Care Act of 2010 (known to many as "Obamacare") was supposed to help Americans with the cost of long-term care. But the Community Living Assistance Services and Supports Act (CLASS) was deemed unworkable and dropped from Obamacare.

So, for the most part, the expense and management of long-term care falls on individuals and their families.

The good news is there are some financial tools you can use to address the cost of long-term care. But you'll need to plan ahead for these strategies to work as intended.

Is Long-Term Care Insurance Worth It?

Investing in long-term care insurance can be expensive. And there's always the chance you won't end up needing it. If you die without going into long-term care, the money you spent on a long-term care insurance policy goes away. Poof!

A different approach that's growing in popularity is a life insurance policy that also includes long-term care coverage through the purchase of an optional rider to the policy. These combination long-term care/life insurance policies (also called "asset-based" or "linked" policies) will cover certain long-term care expenses that regular health insurance or Medicare won't. When you die, whatever money is left in your policy becomes a death benefit for your beneficiaries.

Some life insurance policies now offer what is called an accelerated death benefit, or ADB. This mechanism allows you to receive a tax-free advance on your life insurance death benefit while you are still alive. Depending on the type of policy you have, you can use the accelerated death benefit if you are terminally ill, have a life-threatening diagnosis, are confined to a nursing home, or are in need of other forms of long-term care. The amount of money you use for this kind of care would be subtracted from your life insurance policy's face value.

Here's an example of how an accelerated death benefit would work:

Suzanne has a life insurance policy that includes a tax-free ADB. Her policy is valued at $200,000.

While in her seventies, Suzanne has a bad fall and now needs long-term care, likely for the rest of her life. She can start drawing a monthly accelerated death benefit, which is calculated as a percentage of the total life insurance policy value. The ADB in Suzanne's policy is set at 3 percent, which means she can receive up to $6,000 a month to cover her long-term care costs.

Many life insurance policies make a distinction between nursing home care and less expensive in-home care, according to statistics from the U.S. Department of Health and Human Services. For example, Suzanne's policy may call for $6,000 a month to cover nursing home care, but only $3,000 a month for in-home care. The money you receive from these kinds of policies can vary greatly, but the accelerated death benefit is typically capped at 50 percent of the total death benefit. Some policies, however, will let you use the full amount of the death benefit while you are alive.

If you can't qualify for the insurance, you can also buy an annuity that includes a long-term care rider, usually for an additional annual cost. A "nursing home doubler" annuity, for example, will make double payments for long-term care for up to five years. The disadvantage is that the funding from an annuity would only last that long—which might not be enough time in some cases of long-term care.

A life insurance policy that collateralizes the premium money for long-term care needs can be costly. Typically, you wouldn't necessarily buy this kind of policy until age sixty-five, when the risks of a chronic or terminal illness increase. Unfortunately, when you reach that age, you may not qualify for the insurance or may pay higher premiums due to your age. However, these are effective tools for addressing the escalating cost of in-home or nursing home care. And, unlike long-term care insurance policies, you don't lose the money upon death if you never end up needing long-term care—you won't get your long term care premium back, but your policy's death benefit will still be paid out.

"It'll Never Happen to Me"

As is the case with our own mortality, the prospect of someday no longer being able to care for ourselves seems morbid and depressing. We don't like to talk or think about it. Many of us might not think it will ever happen to us. Sometimes, we might joke about having a "Do Not Resuscitate!" sign over our hospital bed in the event of a dire medical emergency.

In most cases, of course, the answer isn't as simple as pulling a plug. And the statistics suggest that many of us will require long-term care during our lives.

According to statistics from Morningstar Inc., 15 million Americans are expected to need a high level of long-term care by the year 2050. If you're a man turning sixty-five, you have a 46.7 percent chance of needing long-term care during your life. If you're a woman turning sixty-five, that likelihood is 57.5 percent, according to Morningstar's numbers.[25]

Bottom line: The chances are greater than 50-50 that you will need some form of long-term care. Many of us are unprepared for that life event when it happens.

According to National Retirement Institutes' survey on long-term care, more than one in three older adults said they had failed to discuss long-term care insurance expenses with anyone.[26]

We have to get rid of this mentality of "It's not going to happen to me." Long-term care is a real conversation that needs to take place, and the costs are very real. Look everywhere and you'll see the costs are continuing to increase each year.

You may feel healthy as a horse right now. You may have plenty of assets and a sizable nest egg to fund your retirement. You may have done everything right, money-wise, in your life. But who's going to manage that money if you have a terrible accident?

---

[25] Christine Benz. *Morningstar*. August 31, 2017. "75 Must-Know Statistics About Long-Term Care." https://www.morningstar.com/articles/823957/75-must-know-statistics-about-long-term-care

[26] Darla Mercado. CNBC Markets. October 30, 2019. "More than half of adults over 50 would rather die than do this." https://www.cnbc.com/2019/10/30/more-than-half-of-adults-over-50-would-rather-die-than-do-this.html

I have a client who's in his nineties. He owns thirty properties that are going to seed right now because he's in long-term care, living on a feeding tube and a water tube. When we met, we discussed some options. He had some assets he wanted our help with, but he wanted to hold off on all the real estate discussions and talk to his buddy before making any decisions. He's going to lose those real estate assets because he never enlisted a financial partner to help with the responsibility of managing that portfolio. His beneficiaries, his children, never sat down with him to discuss what he owned and where, and he did not leave them a guiding document to detail what needed to be done, how much he owned, or what he wanted them to do. Because he didn't prepare for the possibility of his incapacitation, or his death, when he passes, his children will likely have no idea what's going on. Since he's been in a near-vegetative state for so long, if his children liquidate his properties, it will be for below their previous market value because the homes are in such poor shape. My client's real estate kingdom, which he spent a lifetime building, will vanish in a flash because he didn't have a plan to care for it in the event he was incapacitated.

As you enter your retirement years, not having a strategy to address the possibility of long-term care can lead you to make some desperate and disastrous financial decisions. You do not want to face the prospect of moving into a nursing home that will drain your assets until you qualify for Medicaid. And that's what happens to many elderly Americans. Statics from the SCAN Foundation, a public charity focused on long-term care, show that one in five middle-income seniors will spend enough out-of-pocket money on long-term care to eventually end up on Medicaid.[27]

---

[27] Amada Senior Care. March 2019. "Out-of-Pocket Spending for Senior Care: The Harsh Reality." https://amadaseniorcare.com/2019/03/out-of-pocket-spending-for-senior-care/

This is a last resort that retirees and their families do not want to experience. Medicaid pays for a portion of an estimated 62 percent of all long-term care users. That percentage is only projected to increase.[28]

So, if you're entering your sixties and haven't yet had that not-so-fun conversation about long-term care, do so now—first with your spouse and then with a financial advisor.

You might not believe you'll ever need protection from the significant expenses of long-term care but, to borrow a phrase from *The Hunger Games*, the odds are most definitely <u>not</u> in your favor.

---

[28] Kaiser Family Foundation. June 2017. "Medicaid's Role in Nursing Home Care." https://www.kff.org/infographic/medicaids-role-in-nursing-home-care/

CHAPTER TEN

Climbing Down the Retirement Mountain— Without Breaking Your Neck!

What? You haven't heard about the retirement mountain?

I call it "the retirement mountain" because it sounds better than "going over the hill." In all seriousness, you took a long treck to get to the point of retirement. The accumulation of wealth you have built over time to support your well-deserved retirement was its own journey.

Congratulations, you've made it to your summit. I realize some people's mountains are larger than others, but the logic of retirement planning does not change with the size of the mountain.

People scale the retirement mountain in different ways. Maybe in your case, you used a wealth accumulator, or a money manager. Or perhaps you self-managed your own growth and just hoped for the best. Whatever course you followed, I know it was a hard climb. Now you've reached the summit and are ready to retire after many years of hard work.

How long will you stay at that summit? Well, that's an easy answer. No sooner do you reach the top of the mountain then it's time to head back down. As any mountain climber can tell you, the descent can be tricky. The last thing you want to do as you climb down is to lose money when you retire or, worse yet, run out of money while retired.

How do you safely get down the retirement mountain? Just like with a real mountain, the muscle groups you used to go up are not the same ones you use to go back down.

For starters, you'll need a different skill set. Whether you used a money manager or self-managed your funds on the way up, you'll want to have the added assurance that you won't run out of money during your descent, regardless of market performance.

There are a number of ways to help accomplish this. One strategy is to protect at least a portion of your money from market risk with a fixed or guaranteed financial vehicle. There are numerous options, and you will need to evaluate your unique situation to determine which makes sense for you. One such option is a fixed annuity. You can transfer a portion of your market-based assets to an annuity, often through a process called a "rollover." With the annuity, you will give up some upside potential in case of a bull market, but you won't lose money in a down market and can also add an optional rider for guaranteed lifetime income to your annuity.

This helps provide income for the rest of your life, which assists your climb down the mountain. Some insurance companies offer this rider for as little as .75 percent per year. By purchasing this lifetime income rider, the insurance company will provide a steady stream of income for your remaining years.

Many people choose to put pre-taxed funds into an annuity by rolling over their retirement account, and then, based on the annuity and rider they chose, their money has the potential to accumulate over time.

However, not all income riders are created equal. Some offer bonuses, which involve additional terms and restrictions, while others provide guaranteed percentage interest credits to your annuity's income value. Still other annuities only allow you to draw income after a certain period of time.

An annuity is not your only option for protecting your savings and generating a steady stream of income during your retirement. But it can be part of a balanced approach to managing your money. And an annuity is one of the few vehicles that guarantee you will not lose money from market volatility. All annuity guarantees are backed by the financial strength of the issuing insurance company, so you'll want to do your research on the company before deciding which annuity might be right for you.

Annuities can be a good fit for those who want protection from market volatility, while also wanting their money to grow. But annuities aren't for everyone.

Let's say your income is fine in retirement, and you're not all that concerned with the market being bumpy. That is totally fine. It is okay to be in the market. Ultimately, it becomes a question of, do you want to meet the market or beat the market, knowing you might do neither and could lose money too? Long-term data consistently shows that investing in the market tends to be the most profitable strategy when it's used over a longer period of time.

Three Important Questions

In preparing for your retirement, the first thing you want to do is to simply ask yourself, "Do I want to be exposed to market risk while coming down the mountain?"

If your answer is, "No risk," then you move to the second question: "How much liquidity or access to these funds do I need—some liquidity, mostly liquid, or hardly any liquidity at all?"

You can easily answer this question if you're talking about qualified funds like your retirement savings. Often, liquidity is not a top concern, because these funds are set aside for your retirement years due to the additional tax implications on withdrawals, depending on your age and circumstances when accessing these funds. Also, keep in mind that whatever you withdraw from a qualified plan will be taxed as ordinary income, even if you are over the age of fifty-nine-and-one-half.

The third question to ask yourself is, "Do I want to focus on lifetime income or growth?" This question is important because some people have plenty of retirement income and want the added assurance of their retirement savings' growth potential without risk to market loss, whereas many other retirees will want strategies in place to provide a steady income stream that can help maintain a lifestyle similar to their working years.

Once you've answered these questions to your own satisfaction, it becomes a lot easier to identify the right path for you to take down the mountain.

Again, here's your checklist:

1. Do I want market risk?

2. How much liquidity do I need? A lot, just some, or not much at all?

3. Do I want to focus my retirement funds on income or on growth?

What's the Right Answer?

Of course, the right answer may depend on your specific situation. But one *common* answer to the above questions is, "I want no risk, some liquidity, and I want to focus on income."

Your next step is to sit down with someone who focuses on retirement and not just someone who focuses on portfolio growth. This very well may not be the same financial advisor you currently use. You want to make sure your advisor has a strong knowledge of annuities with income riders and other income products available. These products can change on an almost weekly basis, and keeping up with them can be a full-time job.

The Right Path Down the Mountain

You worked hard going up the retirement mountain. Not everyone makes it to the summit, but you did. This should make you very proud and also excited. However, you'll only be at that summit for a brief period of time, and you'll need to start planning your path down before you make the descent.

Congratulations again on making to the summit. Now, let's prepare for the downhill climb.

CHAPTER ELEVEN

Don't Wait, Don't Procrastinate!

Gen. Douglas MacArthur was one of the greatest military commanders in our nation's history. He rose to the rank of brigadier general in World War I, played a crucial role in our nation's victory in the Pacific theater in World War II, and was mastermind of the brilliant Inchon invasion that turned the tide in the Korean War.

But even a military leader as talented and decorated as MacArthur had some regretful moments.

One of them happened shortly after the Japanese attacked Pearl Harbor in 1941. MacArthur, who was U.S. commander of the Philippines at that time, failed to act on an agreed-upon plan to counterattack the Japanese. In fact, he did nothing at all, allowing the Japanese air force to bomb Clark Field in Manila, destroy the U.S. Far East air fleet, and launch the invasion of the Philippines.

MacArthur's inability to act in the face of immediate danger led to the loss of the Philippines, which the Allies would not reclaim until MacArthur's glorious return in 1944.

Why did the general procrastinate when an attack from the enemy was eminent? No one knows. But it remains a cautionary tale of what can happen to the best of us when we fail to plan ahead and take appropriate action, just hoping instead that disaster won't strike.

Okay—so maybe putting off your retirement planning isn't as drastic as losing the Philippines. Still, it's a strategic blunder I see many people—especially young people—make again and again. They procrastinate. They put things off. They fail to plan ahead.

They don't implement some of the simple but critical lifestyle changes I've outlined in this book, hoping instead to just skim by for as long as they can.

This is not only a matter of money. It's a matter of time. Why do people run out of money during their retirement? One of the key reasons is that they waited too long to begin building their savings. Waiting until your forties and fifties to start thinking about saving for your retirement really puts you at a disadvantage.

Your retirement planning—setting up that 401(k), putting money into a Roth IRA, and budgeting your life appropriately—should really start as soon as your working life begins, as soon as you get your first serious job. Studies have shown that the people who begin investing at least 10 percent of their income while in their twenties are able to accumulate far more wealth than those who start later. That's even true for folks who *stopped* putting as high a percentage of their income into retirement accounts during their later working years.[29]

---

[29] Steven Richmond. Investopedia. November 17, 2019. "Why Save for Retirement in Your 20s?" https://www.investopedia.com/articles/personal-finance/040315/why-save-retirement-your-20s.asp

The difference is the amount of time allowed for that savings to grow.

The Buyer's Market of 1803

Here's another history lesson. One of the all-time greatest land-grabs was the Louisiana Purchase of 1803. The United States purchased that 828,000-square-mile swath of land—which stretched from New Orleans to Montana—from the French for the purchase price of just $15 million.

Adjusted for inflation, that $15 million would have been more like $600 billion in today's dollars. Still, it was considered a great bargain in 1803.

Why would France sell so much territory so cheaply? Well, France's leader, Napoleon Bonaparte, needed the cash to fund his war against Spain—one of many wars he would fight in the ensuing years. Napoleon was one of history's greatest military conquerors, but even he had to make sure his armies and adventures were properly funded.

President Thomas Jefferson used Napoleon's desperate situation as leverage to command a good price for the Louisiana Purchase.

So today, we can thank Napoleon's impulsiveness, aggression, and poor planning for nearly a third of the continental United States. With land values ranging between $1,000 and $4,000 an acre today, the Louisiana Purchase's true value is probably around $1.2 trillion as of right now.

It's another example of how bad timing and a lack of vision can lead to an unfortunate decision. History is filled with these moments.

My goal is for you to not experience your own Louisiana Purchase or, worse yet, your own personal Waterloo.

Those Who Ignore History...

History is a good teacher. You know the old saying about how those who ignore history are doomed to repeat it? It's a popular phrase because it happens to be true—and it tends to happen over and over again.

Still, how do our modern lives relate to what Napoleon or MacArthur experienced?

Here's a common scenario: Jason is in his early fifties, living in New Jersey. His kids are grown and out of college. He and his wife, Flo, live in a four-bedroom home in a solid middle-class neighborhood.

Many people at Jason's stage of life might be thinking about scaling back or downsizing. But Jason has just landed a sweet new consulting job that will more than double his income in less than two years. With no kids at home and fewer responsibilities, Jason and Flo decide now is the time to enjoy the good life. They buy a $950,000 home in that brand-new golfing community across town—the one with the annual homeowners' association fees of $3,000.

Jason also buys that $58,000 Corvette he'd always dreamed of owning. Why not? He is still more than ten years away from retirement and making more money than he ever has in his life.

Here's where the Louisiana Purchase moment comes in. More than a decade passes by. Jason is now ready to leave his consulting job and prepare for retirement. But the housing market, consumer tastes, and the economy have changed since Jason bought that big house off the twelfth tee at Pinewood Estates. McMansions aren't in demand the way they were in the early 2000s, and Jason and Flo may have to sell their home for a fraction of what it was worth when they bought it. Or they can hope the housing market bounces back and continue making mortgage payments until it does. Those payments didn't seem like such a big deal when Jason had his big consulting job. But now, during retirement, they're a major burden.

Jason is also beginning to wish he'd saved more money during his working years instead of making an $800 car payment on that Corvette over the course of seventy-two months. He only gets to drive it with the top down about three months out of the year, due to the New Jersey weather. Most of the time, the car takes up the third bay of Jason's three-car garage, looking like a very expensive, canary-yellow paperweight.

Eventually, the mortgage payments become too much for Jason and Flo to bear, so they sell their big house for $600,000—little more than half of what they bought it for more than ten years ago. That big windfall they envisioned from selling their expensive home never materialized. Like Napoleon and the Louisiana Purchase, they sell their real estate at a massive discount because they need liquidity and to get out from under some of their debt.

It's a common mistake many people make when they get a big promotion or a pay increase late in their working lives. Once you're in the money, it's tempting to buy that dream home or that expensive sports car you've always wanted. But acquiring things that require monthly payments for years on end can be problematic when you decide to retire and scale back your life.

Are You a "MacArthur?"

For every person who decides to drastically increase their cost of living in their forties or fifties, I'd say there are at least three people who take the MacArthur approach when it comes to retirement planning.

In other words, they don't do anything at all. Retirement seems so far away, and there are more pressing concerns to worry about. So they put it off. There'll be plenty of time to save for retirement later, they think.

Brad and Lexie are a bright, young couple in their early twenties who have recently entered the workforce. Brad has a sales job with a freight brokerage. Lexie has a nursing job at the hospital. Both of their employers offer 401(k) plans that will match as much as 5 percent of their income.

"We should really do these 401(k)s," Lexie tells Brad one night after work. "It's basically free money from our companies."

Brad agrees, but he worries about him and Lexie socking away 5 percent of their income when it could be to put to more immediate use. The couple just moved to a nice townhouse in the suburbs, in an award-winning school district. They just bought a new living room set from Nebraska Furniture Mart. The next big purchase will be furniture for a nursery—they're expecting their first baby in May.

With all those expenses and a big change to their lives on the horizon, Brad and Lexie just don't think they can afford to take advantage of their employers' generous 401(k) matches right now. There will be plenty of time to think about that later—maybe a year from now when things have settled down and they're on firmer financial footing. After all, they're both in their early twenties. Retirement is more than forty years away.

The problem with this mentality is that things often *don't* settle down. There will always be expenses—the ones you can anticipate and the ones that pop up out of the blue. Maybe it's an unexpected car repair bill, a new air conditioner for the townhouse, or greater-than-expected daycare expenses for the newborn baby?

Flash forward five years. Brad and Lexie now have two children and are spending $1,600 a month on a highly regarded Montessori day care provider. Both Brad and Lexie have received pay increases from their jobs, but money remains tight. The expenses seem to grow along with their income. At times, it feels like they are living paycheck to paycheck.

And, guess what? They still haven't gotten around to setting aside some of their hard-earned money for the 401(k)s. What seemed like a fairly simple move toward retirement savings five years ago now feels like a significant burden.

Oh, well—they're still in their late twenties. Maybe they'll start budgeting and saving for retirement in a year or so—when things finally settle down?

Brad and Lexie are not alone. An estimated 25 percent of U.S. adults have no retirement savings, according to a 2018 report from the Federal Reserve. Young workers are the least likely to save for retirement—the survey found that 42 percent of respondents who were between eighteen and twenty-nine had no retirement savings at all.

Perhaps even more damning, the Federal Reserve's report found that a third of *all* middle-class adults can't afford to cover a $400 emergency.[30]

In other words, a minor car repair would send a third of the middle class scrambling to find emergency funding.

Talk about living on the edge!

Studies have shown the earlier you start saving for your retirement, the greater your chances of building wealth you can live off of after age sixty-five. For those young people who do invest in 401(k)s, the numbers are fairly promising. According to data from CNBC Make It and Fidelity, twentysomethings who use 401(k) plans contribute an average of 7 percent of their paychecks to their plans. As of early 2019, the average 401(k) balance for people aged twenty to twenty-nine was $11,800.[31]

---

[30] Board of Governors of the Federal Reserve System. May 2019. "Report on the Economic Well-Being of U.S. Households in 2018."
https://www.federalreserve.gov/publications/files/2018-report-economic-well-being-us-households-201905.pdf

[31] Kathleen Elkins. CNBC Make It. July 30, 2019. "Here's How Much Money Americans in Their 20s Have in Their 401(k)s."
https://www.cnbc.com/2019/06/11/how-much-money-americans-in-their-20s-have-in-their-401ks.html

Again, Don't Procrastinate!

When you start saving for retirement in your twenties, time is on your side. So are your daily expenses. Saving between 5 and 10 percent of your income is easier when you're young, when you likely have fewer mouths to feed and other responsibilities. If your employer doesn't offer a 401(k), there are other retirement vehicles, like a Roth IRA. In 2020, you can put as much as $6,000 into a Roth, which is a great tool for avoiding taxation on your future investment earnings.

Having your money automatically deducted for a 401(k) or a Roth IRA with each pay period is the best way to go. After a while, you won't even miss that money, as it slowly builds funding for your retirement.

So, what are you waiting for? Let's get started on a plan for your retirement!

CHAPTER TWELVE
There's No "I" in "Team"

Almost without exception, the difference between winning and losing is having a great team.

We see this in team sports all of the time. Even as we celebrate the athleticism and talent of individual players, we know they can't do it all by themselves. They need a team of reliable, committed coaches and players to win that championship and cut down the nets after the buzzer sounds.

The same approach applies to finance and retirement planning. While many people choose to "go it alone" in planning and preparing for their retirements, they often are not as successful in accumulating wealth and using the available money management tools as those of us who seek out the help of a team of professionals.

Notice how I mentioned "team of professionals" there? That's because, when it comes to effective retirement planning, you really need more than just your insurance agent or your financial advisor who's known you for twenty-some-odd years. Those folks can definitely be valuable resources, but they are just two pieces of the team of advisors you'll need to plot out your successful climb up (and down) the retirement mountain.

I'll have more on that later. First, I'd like to talk a little basketball.

The Jordan Rules

Today there's some debate as to who is the greatest professional basketball player of all time. LeBron James, Steph Curry, and Kobe Bryant certainly have their advocates for the title of all-time best.

Back in the 1990s, though, there was *no question* as to who was basketball's GOAT ("Greatest of All-Time"). It was Michael Jordan, the star shooting guard for the Chicago Bulls and winner of an incredible six NBA championships.

Jordan was such a phenomenal athlete, in fact, that he won three championships with the Bulls, then "retired" to play two seasons of professional baseball, and then returned to the Bulls to win *another* three NBA titles. His last moment on the court for the Bulls came in 1998, when he drained a last-second shot to beat the Utah Jazz in Game Six of the Finals. It was the penultimate moment of what many consider to be one of the greatest sports careers ever.

"Jordan was the most gifted athlete in the league," wrote David Halberstam in his book about Jordan, *Playing for Keeps*. "But unlike most other supremely gifted players, he had an additional quality rare among superb artists whose chosen work comes so easily: He was an overachiever as well."

Still, Jordan wasn't always a champion. For many years with the Bulls, he wore the shameful tag of "Can't Win the Big One." During his first six years of pro ball, Jordan often led the league in scoring, was a fixture at the NBA's annual Slam Dunk Contest, and was, of course, the namesake of the legendary Air Jordan Nike shoe brand.

But the Chicago Bulls were a regular disappointment, often exiting in the early rounds of the NBA playoffs. Rival teams like the Detroit

Pistons even utilized what they called "The Jordan Rules," a strategy of double- or even triple-teaming Jordan, while daring other members of the Bulls to rise up and beat them.

Usually, that didn't happen.

That's because, while Michael Jordan was undeniably great, he didn't have a great *team* around him.

Luckily for him, that began to change with the hiring of new Bulls coach Phil Jackson in 1989. The addition and development of key players like Scottie Pippen, Horace Grant, and John Paxson gave the Bulls a formidable lineup. All of a sudden, Jordan didn't have to carry the team on his back anymore. And Jordan, who was one of the most famously competitive athletes ever known, was happy to share the glory—it meant winning a championship.

It did. After years of near-misses, the Bulls finally broke through in 1991, beating Magic Johnson and the Los Angeles Lakers in five games to win the NBA Finals.

Michael Jordan is just one prominent example of how even the most talented, capable person is limited in what he or she can accomplish without help from a strong team of contributors.

That's true in sports, school, leadership, business—and even personal finance.

It Takes a Team

One thing I always tell my clients right off the bat is that I don't know that much.

That's not false modesty, by the way. In the grand scheme of things, I really know very little.

I am, however, smart enough to hire the best people I can—who *do* know lots of stuff—so that Fitzwilliams Financial can offer the most skilled team of professionals possible for retirement planning.

I've always subscribed to the idea of surrounding yourself with people who are smarter than you. One of the best pieces of advice I ever received was from Thomas Rustici, an economics professor at George Mason who taught me about the Theory of Comparative Advantage. He also told me this: "Do what you do best, and trade for the rest."

In other words, if you're someone who's really skilled at growing oranges, don't just naturally assume your talents and knowledge will apply to growing grapes. It may be a better idea, in some cases, to partner with someone who's really experienced with grapes instead of trying to do it all on your own.

People make this kind of mistake all the time, especially when it comes to personal finance. I cringe a little bit about the do-it-yourselfers and Internet stock day-traders. The Internet, computer software, and Jim Cramer make investing and money management seem like a fun game anyone can win. They put people at ease, downplay the risks that are at stake, and open the door to rookie mistakes that could easily be mitigated or prevented by the help of some experienced professional advisors.

As a classic television ad points out, staying at a Holiday Inn last night might have been a smart move, but it doesn't mean you're all of a sudden a skilled heart surgeon. Just because you're good at one thing, be it engineering, writing code, treating patients or playing professional basketball, doesn't mean you're all of a sudden going to be a wiz at saving and managing money, and planning for retirement.

That's why I advocate the team approach. It's something I envisioned even back when I started Fitzwilliams Financial with my $5,000 investment. I planned on being the quarterback of my team at the firm, but I knew I would need a wide range of specialized professionals to ensure our success. There is simply too much to learn and know about financial planning for one person to master all of it.

What do you think the mega-rich do? Are they putting tens of millions of dollars into the hands of Ed, the friendly broker who runs that little storefront off Main Street and likes to play golf on Fridays? No. They have a team of helpers—lawyers, financial advisors, licensed health care and life insurance agents, and other professionals—all working in tandem to help protect and grow their client's portfolio.

Maybe you don't have that kind of wealth? It doesn't matter. Your $50,000 or $500,000 in retirement savings is just as vital to you—probably more vital—as the fortunes the super-rich can pump into real estate, preferred stocks, and tax shelters on some obscure Caribbean island few people even know about.

Just like they need a team, *you* need a team.

Building the Fitzwilliams Financial Team

My first team member at Fitzwilliams Financial, of course, was my wife, Corrine. Today, she's our marketing director, but she serves a number of roles beyond that description. She holds her life insurance, health, and annuities license in the state of Virginia. Most importantly, Corrine makes certain that our clients receive exceptional service in every interaction they have with our firm. Her personal mission is to help people plan for their retirements in a safe, sensible way.

So, Corrine was the first team member in the early days of Fitzwilliams Financial. Together, we worked to build the business, enlisting a team of agents to bring new business into the firm.

I thought we were doing well, until I had the good fortune of meeting Joel Tabin.

Joel is the regional vice president of Midland National Life Insurance in our area. I first met Joel at a Midland function and quickly identified him as a smart guy who was making more than I was at the time. See, I was making about $250,000 a year but I had a lot of balls in the air. I had about 100 agents writing or trying to write business under my firm while I was personally selling life insurance to help protect new mortgage holders. I would help families ensure their mortgage was taken care of if there was a death, disability or illness.

I was running a hundred miles an hour during the day and well into the night. If I wasn't on the phone with a client or prospect, I was on the phone with an agent discussing their client or prospect.

Joel noticed this and came down to visit me one day to talk business planning with Corrine and me. I invited him to my condominium of 1,200 square feet in the not-so-best area of town. I was doing great, and stacking money into my business hand over fist. I had just opened an office near the local mall (also not in the best area of town).

I wanted to reward myself for this successful start to Fitzwilliams Financial, so I went out and bought a $100,000 Lexus LS460. As I was talking to Joel, I invited him into my life to discuss personal finance. I thought, "This guy makes more than me, what could it hurt?"

At first he was taken aback and surprised, but in classic Joel Tabin fashion, he turned into the Jedi I have come to know. He first said, "Take back the car." I was devastated. He said, "Go buy two nice cars and take back the Lexus."

In my head, I didn't want to listen to him, but my heart and my soul told me, DO IT! So I did. I took back the Lexus and bought two cars. One for me, and one for my wife.

Joel and I then visited my office. I was very proud of my office and my agents. Joel looked at my production reports and started going down the list. I remember this like yesterday, he literally pointed at names on the list and said "bye-bye!" while waving goodbye. That day we cut out about 95 percent of all of my agents. He wanted me to focus like a laser on earning my first $1 million before helping others out in the industry.

Now, as I look back after hitting that milestone, I understand that Joel was completely right. To this day we are great friends and he is like a big brother Jedi to me. I always run my money decisions by Joel no matter if it is business or personal. I wish everyone had a mentor like Joel, someone who tells you like it is, even when it's not pretty. Someone who listens, teaches, and can push you to execute the actions you discuss in mentoring.

This all goes back to my economics training: "You do what you do best, and trade for the rest." This is called comparative advantage by David Recardo. It's funny how, after all these years, some things you just don't forget. It just makes sense.

I took this rule and designed my entire business model around it. I wanted to find people with skills who were better than me in areas that were not my expertise.

Long ago, I quickly realized I was not good at paperwork. I even have a T-shirt that says, "I can close anything except an envelope." So the first person I needed on my team was a top-notch office manager. But how do you hire an office manager to keep up with my ideas and thoughts? For me, the answer is you hire a client. Not just a client, but Deanna Jones, a client who put me through the ringer for about a year straight before she committed her father's last monetary gift to my management. You see, her father had just passed away from cancer and she did *not* want to lose that money, no matter what. She was invited to a seminar by a CPA named Gary Roberson, who I was courting to be our CFO at the time (more on him in a bit).

Now this was one of my first financial seminars. The topic was "Tax-Free Retirement." I packed the house with people I met from grocery store interactions to client referrals to friends. Deanna Jones was in the audience that night. And that night changed her life and mine. The problem was, at the time, I had an employee, I had a manager, but not a true team player.

Over the next year, Deanna questioned me and questioned me until she understood the solution better than most agents understand things in this business. I knew then that as soon as I could, I would hire her for the long run. A year or two later, there was a change in my staff, and so I called Deanna. Today she is my Chief of Operations and runs the logistics of over $100 million in assets.

Now I mentioned Gary Roberson as a CPA I was courting to become my CFO. Well, after a few years of chasing, I was finally able to get Gary to come on board.

I hated taxes. I hated paying taxes. I hated talking about taxes. But I knew it was a necessary topic in my business and one my clients constantly ask about. The idea dawned on me to bring on a CPA/accountant who could help our clients with their taxes and tax questions. Again: "Do what you do best, and trade for the rest."

Jeremy Domozick is our estate planning attorney. He helps our clients with wills, trusts, medical directives, living wills, and any other estate planning needs our clients may require. I have known Jeremy since the third grade. I remember to this day that he sat next to me in class and sometimes he wore a dinosaur sweatshirt.

Jeremy and I both went to George Mason University, and he went on to receive his law degree from William and Mary, one of the top law schools in America. Later in life, we reconnected through our networking. Who would have known that a third grade friend would later become a major part of my business model? It's funny how things sometimes work out that way.

The next person to join the team was Brian Lindberg. I hired Brian to help me with the influx of opportunities we had from our dinner seminars. He was a sales manager at another firm in a different industry. I met Brian at a networking event and quickly noticed he could keep up with me and had a head and heart for fianances. Brian was the man.

Brian has become one of our resident financial advisors, and my right-hand man in the process of building financial strategies.

If you notice, I hand-picked each member of my team to do what I cannot do. I looked for skills in each area where I was weak or not educated enough to give advice. I became the financial quarterback. I became the rainmaker and our team synergy created one place where a client could trust to get all their financial questions answered. I don't answer the phones, I don't recommend investments, I don't craft estate plans, and I'm not a tax professional. My licensing is in insurance solutions, and that is where I specialize and continue to expand my knowledgebase. But together, we all comprise an efficient, effective, and professional team.

Gathering the Best Team

Also crucial to any successful team is having players who may not always agree, but will make the team better. In her book, *Team of Rivals: The Political Genius of Abraham Lincoln*, Doris Kearns Goodwin explains how the president intentionally assembled a cabinet made up of divergent personalities. Three of his cabinet members even ran against Lincoln in the 1860 presidential election.

There was method to Lincoln's madness. His goal was to gather the best possible advisors, regardless of their personal agendas, opinions or their relationships to him. Because of this diversity (and also because Lincoln was so masterful at reading and managing people), the Lincoln Cabinet was arguably the best in our country's history, guiding us through the Civil War, Emancipation, and numerous other crucial issues of those times.

I agree with Lincoln's approach. I, too, want to assemble a team of people who challenge me, educate me, and always advocate on behalf of the constituents—our clients.

With more than ten years behind us at Fitzwilliams Financial, I believe we've gotten off to a good start. But we're always on the lookout for new talent and ideas, all in the name of better serving you, the client.

CHAPTER THIRTEEN

The Green-Light Retirement

We are blessed to live in a prosperous age when a comfortable retirement not only seems plausible for many of us, it has almost become expected.

Go back just a few generations, and the idea of leaving the workforce was a luxury reserved for only the wealthiest members of society. As recently as the early 1940s, the vast majority of Americans were of modest means, and could expect to work hard for as long as they were physically and mentally able. With the Great Depression subsiding and a world war to be fought, the idea of just holding down a job for as long possible was an aspiration for nearly a third of the population that had spent the bulk of the 1930s unemployed.

That all changed, of course, with the post-war economic boom and the rise of the middle class. With much of the rest of the world rebuilding from the war, America was the most prosperous nation on Earth, and Americans began to envision a future where they could enjoy life beyond work.

Today, easing into a comfortable, carefree retirement seems nearly like an American birthright. You turn sixty-five, eat some cake at the office retirement party, and you step away to play golf, go on that two-week Mediterranean cruise, or maybe dedicate yourself to volunteer work or something else you're passionate about. You've reached your golden years, and it's time to do life entirely on your own terms.

It's a dream many of us have, but not one any of us should take for granted. If there's one lesson I'd like you to take from this book, it is this: Planning for retirement requires discipline, patience, and a sound strategy. The risks of not having enough money to retire—or running out of money early in your retirement—are very real. Social Security may not be there for you as a safety net. Taxation on your savings is a major concern. And temptations loom large in the form of heavily marketed schemes that won't work for your situation and could deplete your retirement savings, instead of boosting your wealth.

In other words, planning for your retirement—and sustaining your retirement—is a challenge. It's hard. You can choose to go it alone in saving for retirement if you want. But it helps to have a team of trusted professionals behind you.

A Holistic Approach to Retirement

When people come to see me, it's not unusual for them to not have a complete handle on their full financial picture. A person may know, for example, that he's got $1 million in savings. He'll know he's paying $1,800 a month on his mortgage, and $600 a month on his car. He'll know he faithfully puts 10 percent of his income into his company-sponsored 401(k) with every pay period.

But does he know how much in management fees he's paying on that 401(k)? Does he know what kinds of cost-of-living adjustments he will need to make to offset no longer bringing home a steady paycheck? Does he have a full accounting of his expenses—from grocery bills, to utilities, to the cost of getting the dog groomed once a month and feeding it that expensive, organic pet food the vet recommends?

At Fitzwilliams Financial, we look at all of these elements and more: assets, debt, monthly expenses, cost-of-living adjustments, inflation, Social Security payments, RMDs, fund management fees, pensions, 401(k)s, IRAs, life insurance policies, and more. We'll ask you numerous questions about how you envision your retirement. Do you expect to have a lifestyle and cost of living similar to what you have right now, as a worker? Or do you plan to scale down to a more modest home and lifestyle?

Having a full, clear picture of a client's total wealth and lifestyle enables us to build a retirement plan in real time. We'll implement strategies designed to minimize your exposure to market risk and taxation, and we'll be able to calculate your future income, your expenses, how much you need to live on, and how much money you want to keep growing in a carefully managed, balanced portfolio.

The goal is to create a well thought-out strategy, using a variety of investments, insurance products and services, all designed to help you address your financial needs and concerns.

The strategy we craft for you will have one or more of these three goals:

1. To Grow—You'll prepare for retirement by putting your hard-earned assets to work. This can be accomplished through retirement income strategies, wealth management, annuities, investments, IRA/401(k) rollovers, and other financial tools.

2. To Preserve—The number one concern for many retirees today is that they someday will run out of money. You want to protect the assets that can help you live the retirement you've always wanted. We're able to help you do this through asset protection strategies, life insurance, tax-efficient measures, and long-term care strategies.

3. To Give—Most people don't want to just live off of their wealth, they'd like to pass some of it down to the next generation. We can help you provide for the people and causes you care most about through tactics like IRA legacy planning.

Here's how we get the process rolling for your Green-Light Retirement. In your first meeting with Fitzwilliams Financial, we get to know you. We will fill out a form with all your financial data—from the pension fund, to the mortgage payments, to the regular expenses of daily life. We'll analyze that information, input it into our proprietary financial planning software, and come up with a plan.

In your second meeting with us, we'll share that plan with you, and be able to show you your full financial portfolio in a way you've never seen it before.

This is where the Green-Light Retirement begins.

Red Light, Green Light

Many of us once played the game, "Red Light, Green Light" as kids. The object of the game, of course, was to not get caught when someone yells out, "Red light!"

In the Green-Light Retirement plan, "red" isn't necessarily bad, but it does symbolize risk to your assets that you'll want to be mindful of as you enter your retirement years.

During your second meeting with Fitzwilliams Financial, we'll present you with a graphic that illustrates your full financial picture, and the level of risk your portfolio is facing. The graphic will look something like this:

DESIRED ALLOCATION

PORTFOLIO TOTAL
$1,075,000

- LOW RISK — 61.00%
- AT RISK — 34.00%
- EMERGENCY FUNDS — 5.00%

In the graphic, all the money that's protected from market volatility is green—shown here in the darkest shade. All the money that's dependent on the ups and downs of the economy or the stock market is red—shown here as the lightest shade. It's a clear, simple way to fully understand where you're at financially and how vulnerable your assets are to uncertainty.

How much risk should you take? Well, that depends a lot on your age. The classic formula—which is a general rule of thumb only - is to take your age and subtract it from 100. The number you come up with is the recommended level of high-risk, high-reward investments that can be part of your portfolio. For example, if you're forty years old, you can have 60 percent of your assets in riskier ventures. You're relatively young, and you still have plenty of years left to make up for any unexpected drops in the market.

As you get older, of course, you should be a little more careful and risk-adverse in your money management. If you're sixty-five, and you subtract your age from 100, then you know that it's okay to have 35 percent of your assets in higher-risk investments like equities or real estate. The bulk of your assets, however, should typically be shielded in more conservative investment vehicles.

Here's a hypothetical case for us to study. Harold is sixty years old. His assets total $2 million. About 60 percent of Harold's total portfolio is invested in the stock market and in speculative real estate. Here's what Harold's Green-Light Retirement graphic looks like:

CURRENT ALLOCATION

PORTFOLIO TOTAL
$1,075,000

- LOW RISK — 0.00%
- AT RISK — 95.35%
- EMERGENCY FUNDS — 4.65%

What would we tell Harold about his portfolio? Is it too risky?

Yes. It appears that Harold got the formula wrong about age and risk assumption. Being sixty doesn't mean having 60 percent of your assets tied to the market. It means 60 percent of Harold's portfolio should be shielded from risk, in products like life insurance, annuities or perhaps bond funds that are less affected by volatility in the market.

In other words, at least 60 percent of Harold's portfolio should be green (the darkest shade—which you'll notice isn't present at all on Harold's Green-Light circle), but it's okay for as much as 40 percent of it to be red.

Enlisting Fitzwilliams Financial's help and getting a customized Green-Light Retirement assessment doesn't mean you're home-free to a happy retirement. But it sets the baseline of where to begin planning for retirement, and it outlines steps you need to take to help ensure your wealth is protected.

Like a good physician, I encourage my clients to schedule regular check-ups with me—either on a yearly or a quarterly basis. It's a good way for you and for us to keep track of your portfolio's performance, and determine what adjustments need to be made to keep your financial risks under control.

The Ultimate Goal? A Balanced Approach

There's a science to effectively managing your money and planning for a happy retirement. But it's not rocket science. The Green-Light Retirement graphic is a simple way of communicating a fairly simple idea—that you need a balanced, diversified approach to saving and protecting your money.

Every so often, we'll read in the newspaper about a financial collapse that destroyed peoples' lives. In 2002, it was Enron and WorldCom, over-leveraged, publicly-traded companies that went bust, laid off all their employees, and destroyed thousands of people's retirement savings. In 2008, we learned about Bernie Madoff's Ponzi scheme, a massive fraud that ripped off an estimated $64.8 billion from 4,800 clients. Once again, many people lost most or all their retirement savings when Madoff's scheme collapsed.

What do the "innocent" people whose lives were irreversibly changed by these financial disasters have in common? They invested too much of their wealth into one company, or even one person. They weren't diversified. They didn't have a balanced portfolio and, as a consequence, they got burned. Badly.

Taking an all-in approach to money management is never a good idea, whether it's a stock, a mutual fund, a second home or life insurance. And while diversification can't guarantee a profit or ensure you won't have a loss, you need a disciplined, diversified approach across a range of investments and financial products. It's not the easy play, but it's the smarter play.

All my life, I've seen people suffer the effects of poor planning and financial neglect, as well as calamities they had absolutely no control over. I've shared some of their stories with you in this book.

I don't want to see that happen to you. I want you to be able to save for and experience the retirement you deserve. I want to help you shield your assets from whatever misfortunes might happen to you in the coming years. What does your financial picture look like? What are your goals? What do you want your life to look like in ten, fifteen, or twenty-five years?

Give me a call, and let's get together to come up with a plan.

TIMOTHY FITZWILLIAMS

About the Author

As founder and CEO of Fitzwilliams Financial, Timothy Fitzwilliams' passion for helping others stems from his own family's experience. During his early years, he watched his father struggle with medical issues and insufficient insurance coverage from his military retirement, causing financial strain for the family. The circumstances gave him firsthand knowledge of the importance of good financial planning and inspired him to help others create financial confidence through strategic asset protection.

Timothy has more than a decade of experience in the financial services industry and is a Million Dollar Round Table (MDRT) member.[32] A sought-after speaker, Timothy frequently presents informational seminars on tax-free retirement income and Social Security strategies. He is a frequent contributor to a variety of media

---

[32] Million Dollar Round Table ("MDRT") is a membership organization. Qualifying criteria for membership include attaining specified levels of commissions earned, premium paid or income earned on the sale of insurance and other financial products. The MDRT membership requires the payment of annual dues, compliance with ethical standards, and to be in good standing with an MDRT-approved professional association.

outlets, including Fortune, CNN Money, Fox News, ABC, CNN, CNBC, and the Virginian-Pilot.

Timothy holds his life, health, and annuities licenses in multiple states. A graduate of George Mason University, Tim was invited to study at the University of Oxford and the University of Cambridge before graduating magna cume laude with a Bachelor of Science in economics.

Family means everything to Timothy. He and his wife, Corrine, live with their two sons, Timmy and Luke, and Corrine's mother in Chesapeake, Virginia. Timothy's mother is also close by in detached "in-law quarters." An Eagle Scout, Timothy enjoys spending time leading Cub Scouts, volunteering at his church and participating in taekwondo.

Acknowledgments

This book and the work of Fitzwilliams Financial, would not have been possible without help from the following.

I want to thank God first and foremost for all of my blessings. I would like to thank my mother for always encouraging me to do my best and for teaching me to always find the good in things. You taught me to never give up and to always strive for what you want. Mom, no matter what sickness you endured, you always made sure I was able to achieve my goals.

Thank you to my father, who taught me key lessons of life that I use in business every day, my favorite being the phrase, "Work smarter, not harder." Dad, even though you are not here with me, I know you can read this from above.

Thank you to Joel Tabin for being there with me as a mentor and good friend. Your involvement in my life has helped me steer through many difficult situations, from hiring to firing, to firm changes and relationships.

I would also like to thank my very first economics professor. Dr. Carl Rustici. You showed me a world I never knew existed. You taught me how to "look through the peephole in the fence." For that,

I am forever grateful and have used your teachings day in and day out.

Thank you to all of my clients for believing in me and trusting my firm to guide and help you. I could not have done it without you and I am eternally grateful. You changed my life and allowed me to provide for my family in a way I never thought was possible.

To my two sons: You give me the fire to keep burning. Don't think for a minute this will just be passed along with no effort on your part! Remember, boys, "Nothing worth having is easy to obtain."

To my wife: As I have stated many times, you are the backbone of my life, both personal and business. I love you and I appreciate you always supporting and believing in me. I remember like it was yesterday driving to Richmond to make sales calls, and you would stay in the back of the car doing paperwork while I was in the house helping families protect their mortgages.

Last but not least, to Abe Abich: You are one of my best friends and the reason I am in this business. You saw something in me and pushed me toward this career. You knew this was for me, and you never gave up trying to get me in this industry.

Each and every one of you have touched me and crafted me into who I am today. I love you all and appreciate everything you have done and continue to do for my success.

Contact Us

If the topics and themes discussed in this book resonated with you, and if you'd like to employ our team-based approach for your retirement strategy, give us a call and we'll see what we can do:

CONTACT US
Phone: 757.961.0700
Fax: 757.961.0701
Email: tim@ffinancial.net
Virginia Insurance License #127870

CHESAPEAKE OFFICE
860 Greenbrier Circle
Suite 305
Chesapeake, VA 23320